Holy Unexpected

Holy Unexpected

My New Life as a Jew

Robin Chotzinoff

PublicAffairs™

A Member of the Perseus Books Group

Library of Congress Cataloging-in-Publication Data
Chotzinoff, Robin.
    Holy Unexpected : my new life as a Jew / Robin Chotzinoff.
        p.   cm.
    ISBN-13: 978-1-58648-308-1 (hardcover : alk. paper)
    ISBN-10: 1-58648-308-0 (hardcover : alk. paper)
    1. Chotzinoff, Robin—Religion.   2. Jews—United States—
Biography.   3. Bat mitzvah.   I. Title.
E184.37.C56A3   2006
296.7'15092—dc22
[B]

                                                    2006019268

First Edition
10 9 8 7 6 5 4 3 2 1

For Coco and Gus Dexheimer
Diamond Souls

Contents

A Note from the Author

When I talk about God, I almost always say "he," with a small *h*. It's simpler that way. You could go crazy writing "he/she/it" all day.

This is not the story of my entire life, or even the outline, but only the parts that have some relevance to religion. I left a lot out. I hope that doesn't insult anyone.

Introduction

"I hear you snuck off to *shul*," my dad says. "Why?"

"It was *Shabbes*," I say. Then I realize that even if he understands the word, he'll pretend he doesn't.

"It was what?"

"*Shabbes*. Friday night. The Sabbath for Jews, when—"

"Yeah, yeah. So you're still mixed up in that?"

For six years now. Unlike the Tibetan Buddhist summer, the year of carrying a briefcase, or my entire first marriage, Judaism doesn't seem to be a passing fad.

"Religion is for stupid people," my father observes. "Didn't I tell you that?"

"You did," I say. "Lots of times."

"It's a crutch."

"Definitely."

"If there were no religion, everyone would get along better. I wish it had never been invented," he says, now sounding a little desperate.

"I know. You're probably right." And he may be. On the TV news broadcasting soundlessly above his hospital bed, people are throwing stones and Molotov cocktails at each other for semireligious reasons. I've always wondered if this is what Mohammed or the ancient Rabbis had in mind. Nevertheless, I'm a religious person. Indeed it could be I need a crutch.

"So what the hell else is happening?" my dad asks, not for the first time.

He's trying to recover from a heart attack and the partial amputation of his foot, a few of the end results of the fifty years he spent single-mindedly wrecking his health. My sisters and I have been in and out of hospitals almost constantly in the past three years. We know the security guards, the parking scams, how to get doctors to call us back. Dad makes friends with the nurses and waits for us to bring in Chinese, or the deli sandwiches of his New York youth. (This isn't quite possible in Denver, but we try.) We know the drill.

This time, he seems feebler. He no longer asks for the pocket-size vodka bottle. He doesn't remember the last time he wore garments that didn't tie up the back. He's easily tired, but hungry for news of the outside world.

"What's *new* ?" he asks, with a touch of urgency.

What can I tell him? Before sundown yesterday, I sharpened all the knives in the house. According to the *Code of Jewish Law,* published in 1924 by something called the Congregation Sons of Israel 30th Dinner Dance Committee, this is one of several hundred ways to prepare for the Sabbath. Unlike cleaning the house from top to bottom—*ha!*—the knife thing appeals to me. My Chinese cleaver took the kind of edge that falls through a ripe tomato like a guillotine. You could call this a blessing, especially if you like to cook, which I do. Or if your father, who prefers to buy only presents that plug in, bought you the very best Chef's Choice knife sharpener.

"I used your knife sharpener yesterday," I say, deliberately omitting the blessing part. This is a meager gossip item, but at least it doesn't force him to think about God, who has always pissed him off. You can be a Jew without believing in God, and he is—the first-generation American child of Jewish musicians. He knows ten times more Yiddish than I do, cranks out vats of chopped liver, and makes generalizations about the *goyim*. Mel Brooks. Smoked sturgeon. Loud emotions. He's that kind of Jew. "Jew," as he has often pointed out, is a racial classification. If you are one, you don't get to opt out. So you're proud of it. Up to a point.

You stop with all the Jewishness when God enters the picture. You put your foot down at peasant superstition—the Orthodox Judaism personified by his grandfather, my great-grandfather Rabbi Moshe Baer Chatsianov. (After Ellis Island, he became Chotzinoff.) Moshe Baer stood against everything his children loved—art, literature, politics, music. Life itself! Back then, at the turn of the twentieth century, you could either have all that, or you could have stifling, conventional Judaism. You couldn't do both. No one did.

According to this tradition, I was raised a born-again atheist. This was our creed: Religion—who needs it?

I do.

I GET A LOT of questions about proof. My relatives see me as a reasonably intelligent person, so if I'm going to believe in something, I should at least be able to substantiate it. My sister Jenny brings up a story in last month's *Newsweek* about how the tendency to religious belief may well be genetic. She's willing to believe that my brain chemistry enables me to see something that isn't there, and if I want to do that, more power to me. She admires the no-nonsense moral code by which she believes we religious Jews run our lives. Also, she thinks religion can be good for kids.

Well, I'm not the Jew my sister thinks I am. I don't live by a stringent moral code. I don't have a heightened sense of right and wrong just because I've read the Old Testament. Furthermore, I eat bacon, sing Protestant hymns, and collect Zuni religious fetishes. Once I tried to refrain from driving on the Sabbath and got so stir-crazy I almost lost my mind. Long before sundown that Saturday, I was behind the wheel of a minivan, headed for Wal-Mart. I don't care if anyone else wants to be a Jew, or what religion they are or aren't. It might be the first private thing in my life so far.

"That's *farkakteh*," my father decides, using a Yiddish word meaning "worthless," or, literally, "be-shitted." "And tell me one more time how you can believe there's a God when there's absolutely no scientific proof at all?"

"No proof," I agree.

I stopped caring about proof so long ago I have trouble making the connection between God and scientific inquiry.

I'M NEW TO this, but here are three Jewish things I do:

I say a blessing before dinner. We thank God for bread—not so much because it exists, but for the partnership it represents. God makes wheat, we turn it into bread.

I send my kids to Hebrew school. Every morning I read a little Hebrew myself.

I worry. The small, affluent town where I live has room for only one crazy/homeless person at a time. Last summer it was an emaciated young man in a pink quilted lady's raincoat. He suffered intensely from mental illness—I could tell from the way his lips moved as he talked to himself, sweat pouring from his face on a hot summer day, still wearing that coat. He stayed only a few weeks. Where is he? What should have been done? Can you make a person take medication when they don't want to?

Jews are arrogant. God has told us it's our job to repair the world.

Jews are argumentative. If you're going to repair the world, you have to do more than throw on a patch—and who can agree about what that means?

Jews think about food a lot. I should have at least fed that skinny, crazy boy. Would it have killed me to keep a sandwich in the car?

MY FATHER WILL never be able to understand what happened to his proper atheist daughter, and I've quit trying to explain it to him. When I try to explain it to myself, this is the only image that works:

I was standing in an empty swimming pool. I enjoyed the empty space. There was a lot to do in there. I was somewhat surprised when a small amount of water began to trickle in through the cracks. The water is best described as an awareness of God. Over a long period of time, more and more water accumulated until I could no longer touch the bottom and was lifted up. I've been floating ever since. Sometimes this gives me a stoned feeling. Other times I'm too preoccupied to notice.

People point out that there's no water in the pool. In fact, water is practically invisible—a colorless substance that takes on the pigment of whatever it's around. I wish I could flick a wet hand at them, forcing a few drops to land on their skin, but the metaphor doesn't extend that far. Besides, why would I want to convince other people of anything? I hear God loves people who do that, but I don't buy it.

Nevertheless, no matter how much it looks as if I'm standing on a slab of concrete at the bottom of an empty swimming pool, I'm floating.

What I Believed in
Before I Believed in God

At a recent Torah study, we got into a discussion of God's most private name, translated from Hebrew as Y-H-W-H. Our rabbi, Jamie Arnold, admitted that although no one knows what the hell that's supposed to mean, you could think of it as the noise of a deep breath. I liked that.

Those things I believed in before this "breath" were much more confusing. Tricky, even. I often thought the various demigods who appeared to me when I was young were smarter than I was. Sometimes they wielded absolute power over me. Other times I was able to tell them to get lost. Or they were other people's gods and I couldn't make them fit me.

But the fact is, I never was a very convincing atheist.

A LONG TIME ago, I believed in Jesus. For about two hours.

One summer day when I was four, my mother was talking on the black wall phone in the kitchen of our apartment at 88th Street and West End Avenue in New York City, and I had nothing to do. It was strange to be in the city—we usually lived in a rented house on Long Island during June, July, and August. Perhaps my mother was talking to a painting contractor or a divorce lawyer. I can only guess what business brought her into the city with me but without my three-year-old sister, Jenny.

The apartment looked different with no one living in it. The living room furniture was covered with sheets, the shades were pulled down, and the carpets lay rolled up and covered with brown paper, end to end, down the long hallway that led to our bedrooms. The half-lit, shadowy rooms looked almost ominous, reflected in the mirrors my mother put up wherever she lived. The big mirror at the end of the long hallway made it look twice as long. My father had suggested he possessed the power to put us on the other side of this particular mirror, and would do it if we asked. There was just one glitch—he wasn't sure he could get us back. Jenny and I were both adventurous. We'd had several absorbing discussions during bubble baths about whether or not to accept the challenge of the mirror. We hadn't said yes or no yet.

I began to walk down the length of the rolled-up carpets in the hall, watching myself in the mirror, hearing the crunch of brown wrapping paper under my Buster Brown shoes. *Look at me go! I'm balancing! Can I tightrope like this, all the way to the end of the carpet? The tension is terrible, but yes! I can! I'm brave! If I'm brave, I'm probably famous. If I'm famous, I could be Hercules, the cartoon strongman on the* Romper Room *kids' show, throwing thunderbolts around and saving people.*

While people admired Hercules, however, they didn't feel sorry for him, and that's what I wanted. *I could fall off this twenty-foot roll of carpet and end up with a cast on my leg, and then I would be not just brave, but pitiable. What a combination!* And now that I thought of it, my choice was clear—I'd be Jesus. Even kids who'd never been to church knew a rudimentary version of the Jesus story. Nails were driven into his hands and feet. He was a martyr *and* he was famous. That was more like it.

I was Jesus, bravely balancing and occasionally falling off the carpet roll. It was a good game to play alone or possibly with a friend, except that the rules would have to be clear at the start: Only one person would get to be Jesus, and that person would be me. I didn't know who anyone else would get to be because I'd already used up all my Jesus information. Did he have sisters? Neighbors?

That fall, I entered nursery school at Riverside Church, but I don't remember any mention of Jesus. We sang hymns like "All Creatures of Our God and King," but we also sang "Little Red Caboose" and various Peter, Paul, and Mary hits. There were at least fifty tricycles on the roof playground, and we liked to roar around into a snarling gridlock. I didn't have time to think about Jesus anyway. I was busy with my new best friend. Chris Kobin was another secular half-Jewish-on-his-dad's-side New York kid. (Our relationship was brief then, but in the mid-1990s Chris's father married my mother, of all people. Chris and I picked up where we'd left off thirty years before, laughing unto the point of snorting. Sometimes you have to wonder about fate.)

Even if Jesus was just a story to me, I began to get that he was real to other people. They didn't mind getting dressed up on Sunday morning in order to go say howdy to him when everyone else was lying around in pajamas. In the mid-1960s, dress-up for girls meant little white gloves and a sort of purse-size mini-mantilla made of lace.

I had a Catholic friend, and when she spent the weekend with us we had to promise her mom that she wouldn't miss Mass. I went with her on a half-dozen occasions, arriving curious and leaving bored. (The service, conducted mostly in Latin, seemed endless, but it lasted only half as long as the shortest of the synagogue services I attend now.)

At a small stone church in New Jersey, Jesus was a plaster statue with lifelike bloody wounds who looked up at the ceiling as if to ask his Father, "Are you sure this is what you had in mind?" His mother, Mary, was nearby, holding the infant version of her son. The other statues, all in long robes and halos, were saints. That much Molly had told me. Their eyes looked empty, as if their souls had ducked out to get a snack in a back room.

I was clear that these beings, or whatever they were, had been known to speak to people. Not to make normal conversation, either, but to announce miracles and destinies and that sort of thing. So if God or any of his agents wanted to appear during Mass, I was up for it. And the quiet in the room, the beams of sun coming in from the east, the holy water fonts, the blood and body of Christ—which were frankly macabre, so I filed them away to think about later—all gave me the impression that something big was about to happen.

Nothing happened. Molly said nothing ever really did, but that didn't bother her. She believed in God for the long haul and went to church every Sunday, the same way my mother had her

1960s hair re-teased every week at the hairdresser's. Not to trans-form herself, but to stay the same.

Then the priest switched to English. The Christians, he said, are the salt of the earth. Without them, there would be no flavor, nothing much to taste. I was indignant. Of course this wasn't any more arrogant than the "chosenness" of Jews, but I didn't know about that yet. I got mad at the priest. I wouldn't look at him on the way out. Jesus people were by no means more flavorful than anyone else, I thought. Maybe less.

Few known Christians hung out around my family, and my parents explained that this salt thing was a good example of the problem with religious people. They thought they knew some-thing we didn't. And would they ever shut up about it? No. They wanted to save you even if you were perfectly happy unsaved. You had to be quite firm with them. Now I understood the family's po-sition on religion: We were outwardly polite about it, but in-wardly found it *mishuggenah.*

It was okay to admire the pageant of Christmas, though, to allow yourself a shiver at the "shepherds watching their flocks by night" and a star of wonder appearing in the east. My mother made the season almost magical for Jenny and me. We sang carols and made special trips to gaze upon department store windows. Every Christmas morning, stockings appeared on our bedposts, always with oranges crammed into their toes. When I was little and had never experienced a mall, Christmas was the perfect holiday, without one iota of Christianity to muddle it up.

WHEN MY MOTHER went into labor with me, my father brought her to the hospital on his BSA motorcycle. Right before I was born, I experienced kicks and speed. That's what my father says, and it pleases me tremendously, though I'm not sure it's true.

My first word was "cookie."

Motorcycles, bakery items, and family—heavy foreshadowing. After the brief interludes of Jesus, other gods began to appear, first in the form of two old, bald, dead men named Samuel.

It began with a bas-relief bronze head of Samuel Brearley, who founded the Brearley School, a private girls' institution attended by generations of New York women, including my mother, my sister, and me. During assemblies, I would stare at the bronze head off to the side of the stage near the American flag, the velvet curtain, and Miss Mitchell, in the black graduation robes she seemed to wear all year round.

Samuel looked out on a sea of girls in blue uniforms, searching for excellence. I wanted him to be particularly pleased with me. At first, all that meant was sitting up straight, looking like someone who tries hard and succeeds in school (which I was). Gradually, I learned that Brearley girls were supposed to study well, venture into the unknown, and continue to come up with ways to be a modern woman. Ideally, they'd also be good at bombardment or dodgeball, play a leading role in the seventh-grade Gilbert and Sullivan operetta, or win a prize for writing or reciting poetry. Brearley had certain avenues to social success, but my Samuel didn't care about that. He wanted scholars—intelligent, but with pep. He measured me with grades and might have the power to single me out for a really good destiny. He curbed my weirdness with structure. He was very comforting and, with the exception of dodgeball, I was a good Brearley girl.

As early as kindergarten, I liked to think Samuel Brearley was *up above.* From there, he looked *down,* watching over me and the rest of his tribe of little women.

Sometime during that first fall at Brearley, I was playing Chinese checkers with my sister when my father told us that *his* father, Samuel Chotzinoff, had just died of leukemia. Details were fuzzy—could my parents already have been dressed in black for some kind of funeral? Wasn't the family too cosmopolitan for a funeral, and wouldn't it have been a cocktail party tribute instead?

Either way, I started to cry loudly, even though I didn't know my grandfather all that well. Jenny just sat there feeling inadequate. I was now cemented as the *emotional one*, which made her *cold, rational,* and *unfeeling,* since we'd already been pegged as opposites.

Not long after my grandfather's death, I came home from school to find my father standing in the lobby in his jeans and cowboy boots, tears dripping from beneath his aviator sunglasses, holding his brown leather traveling bag. Telling me things that were none of my business had always been his specialty—showing me my Christmas presents right after Thanksgiving, for instance—and now he violated his agreement with my mother and told me he was moving out because they were getting a divorce.

"She'll get over this," he said, delusionally. "We'll get back together soon."

My parents had had a crummy marriage—my few memories of them together involve tense arguments in the car. So my mother was free at last. She hired female college students to live with us as part-time nannies and went to work as a secretary for the Society of Magazine Writers, and we visited our dad on weekends.

I decided to become the man of the house, which meant sitting in my father's chair at dinner, slamming down my fist, and running from the table, as he did, annoying my mother and making her feel trapped, as he did, and complaining about the nonexcellence of the food, as he did.

But all food was nauseating to me at the time—tomato soup that had formed a skin, runny fried eggs, rubbery cold cuts. The smell of the lower school lunchroom was enough to turn me pale green. I became the only kid in my class ever to be allowed to bring lunch from home, and the same lunch every day: an American cheese sandwich on white bread, wrapped in silver foil. In pictures from those days I'm rather skinny, with big knees.

Because everyone knows broken homes and dead grandfathers are traumatic, I went through a sort of Edgar Allan Poe phase, crayoning pictures of graveyards and writing precocious little stories about funerals. Clearly, I needed authority—someone or some thing that would explain the rules and the roles.

I embraced the mythology of my grandfather, who'd been born somewhere in Eastern Europe on the Fourth of July. I memorized the picture of him holding his three granddaughters on his knees, wearing a captain's hat from a drugstore. He was disarming—everyone called him "Chotzie," even the guys who wrote his many obituaries. He hadn't acted important in front of me, but I knew he was and that it had something to do with all the people with Russian accents who hung around his house drinking cocktails and eating clams and playing cards, like regular folk, but then taking out violins, violas, and cellos and inspiring a reverent hush. Children were to remain quiet during these informal concerts.

I knew he had written books—his last published volume was one-third dedicated to me—and that the books told the story of his childhood on the Lower East Side and his love affair with music. Everyone knew he was married to the sister of Jascha Heifetz, the most famous violinist in the world at the time. Uncle Jascha was temperamental. Nervous energy ran through our family whenever he came east. I overheard discussions about whether or not he would agree to see certain people who were falling all over themselves to see him, about what, exactly, he would eat. His genius overrode the annoyance. I remember standing in his dressing room in Carnegie Hall in an itchy velvet dress and mary jane shoes that swallowed up my bobby socks as I walked. Uncle Jascha didn't acknowledge my presence, which was a relief.

Samuel Chotzinoff stood for *family* the way Don Corleone stood for *Mob*. He was my heritage. He made something of himself and expected me to do the same. Like Samuel Brearley, he was up there looking down on me.

NEXT CAME THE goddess of internal combustion. I still think of her as Vroom.

Both halves of my family spent summers in Hampton Bays, Long Island. My mother lived in a three-story shingled beach cottage on Shinnecock Bay, less than a mile from the ocean. My father lived a few miles away on his fishing boat at the Hampton Boat Works. It was easy to travel between the two. By the time I was ten, I could do it by bike.

Hampton Bays wasn't a legitimate Hampton back then. It was unpretentious and affordable. I learned just about everything important there—how to grow tomatoes, how to get a library card, how to bodysurf, how to sail, how to listen to your favorite music while tinkering alone in a garage.

One day, not long after I learned to read, I began to feel compelled to write things down, or at least to remember overheard conversations. I started doing this in Hampton Bays because everything was more worth noticing there.

On my seventh birthday, I looked out of the window and saw a large package tied to a tree. It turned out to be a rope hammock, and it was mine. You could sit in it, swinging and looking up through the lacy foliage of two locust trees, dreaming about this and that. Jenny and I stayed there, even when it started to rain and our Danskin shorts-and-shirt sets were soaked through and we had fallen out of the hammock so many times we were smeared with mud. Then we ran, dripping, to the upstairs bathroom and piled into the claw foot tub with its red painted toenails, even though there wasn't quite enough room for us both.

Clean, dressed in holey jeans and Keds worn to the texture of velvet, I lounged on my bed, reading library books and wondering what was for dinner. A wonderful smell wound its way up to the second floor. Could it be Rice-A-Roni, the San Francisco treat? Willow tree branches snapped against the window glass and rainwater rattled down the gutter downspout that clung to the side of the house with the help of vines. You could grab it for support while sneaking out after dark to a meeting of the Quilties—neighborhood kids who assembled in the empty lot next door, wrapped in blankets or bedspreads. The object of the club was to run around at night in a cape like a superhero.

I lived among people, but it was my world and I memorized its details—the smell of limey vodka tonics drunk by grownups, a worn-out bathing suit on the clothesline in the sun. Roses, dew, lilacs, mildew. Lawnmower cuttings drying on the grass in rows.

I had a composition notebook, just like Harriet the Spy. I drew a lot of horses and princesses in its pages, but also described hydrangeas almost past their bloom, the buzz of giant honeybees my dad called 747s, yelling over the AM radio at a volleyball game at the Coast Guard station, fog horns at night on Shinnecock Bay. The way the light from a buoy shines on the water at night, making a very obvious path from it to you.

I remember a guy named Duck who worked at the Hampton Boat Works and seemed to spend hours repairing boats and talking about cars. I sat up on the flying bridge listening to him. *Camaro . . . Trans Am . . . Mustang . . . dual hemi . . . chopper . . . outboard/inboard . . . Johnson . . . Evinrude . . .*

Over the *chung-chung* of the engine of the 46-foot Hatteras that my father coveted came the whine of the minibikes ridden by neighborhood boys and the tinny outboard motor sound of the boats for rent across the creek at Frank's Fishing Station. If you needed to go to Freeport for parts, you grabbed the keys to the El Camino off the hook and went. Once I was riding with Duck in this car and noticed a rusted hole so big you could see the highway pass by.

Writing was elemental, like scratching. It wasn't somber. It wasn't reverent. I didn't have to do it the way the Samuels did it.

It was liftoff, and I did it by myself, but I wasn't the only one.

Lots of people seemed to have to write. It didn't always make them happy. They did it anyway, alone in a room with a typewriter, an electric, expensive one if they'd been successful. My stepfather, a prolific freelance magazine writer, wrote from early morning until cocktail hour, churning out stories full of numbers, instructions, and bulleted lists, particularly in the areas of marriage and sex. Nine lessons learned from today's sex therapists. Six strategies for blending a stepfamily. On the eve of his marriage to my mother, his fifth wife, he came out with a book called *How to Stay Married,* but after twenty years, they divorced.

The writing he did was work, twice as hard as putting on a suit and taking a cab to a law firm, as other people's fathers did.

"When I write," he once explained to me, "it's as if I'm putting beads on a string. One bead after another. And when something interrupts my concentration, like you playing that violin, or clinking those ice cubes, I have to start all over with different beads and another piece of string."

When you grew up, you had to support yourself and God knows who else. Writing for no particular reason irked my stepfather a lot.

"I suppose you write down whatever comes into your head?" he'd ask.

I did, of course.

"And how do you plan to do that for a living?"

It was a good question and exciting to contemplate. My way of being a working writer would be nothing like his.

I imagined going into Callahan's luncheonette on the inlet in Hampton Bays, with fishing trawlers at the docks unloading their nets under a cloud of seagulls. Inside would be the usual signs on slabs of varnished wood: *Old fishermen never die, they just can't raise their FISHING pole.* Honey Callahan, so old his cheeks sunk in where his teeth should have been, was in love with Jenny—embarrassingly, appallingly in love. He told her she looked like Alice in Wonderland. He bought her heart-shaped boxes of chocolate. It would be my job to write this down, never mind that by then my sister would no longer be nine years old, and Honey would probably be dead. After writing down what happened and eating my cheeseburger, I would go out to my car and drive off somewhere to write about something else.

Perhaps on the way I would see Albert, the only retarded person in town, who got where he was going on a rusty tricycle. He had the face of a baby, sprinkled with five o'clock shadow.

"I'll go places and write about what happens," I told my stepfather.

"You can't do that," he said, and I thought, *Oh no? We'll just have to see about that.*

My father also wrote. He had once made a living as a New York nightlife writer. He hadn't had an audience or an editor in years, but still he cranked out long letters, not just to old friends who'd moved away but to people he saw almost every day. And one summer, still wallowing in divorce misery, he wrote an entire novel about two girls not unlike Jenny and me, who traveled the world in a boat belonging to their father, who'd been kidnapped by dark forces. Every time we saw him, he'd have another ten pages. Being the kind of writer whose imagination keeps on working long after the book is finished, my dad filled us with visions of movie rights and best-seller lists. He typed and typed until the manuscript was more than 300 pages long. Then he put it into a manila envelope, sent it off to a friend of a friend in the publishing business, and waited for the good news.

We didn't understand the rejections. Dad was connected to people in publishing, people who *wanted* to like his writing. They ended up regretting that it was *not for us. Not at this time.* Writing, therefore, was unfair. There were people who wrote only for themselves—Emily Dickinson, say. But my dad wasn't one of them. He put the manuscript away in a drawer where it still sits, the pages now yellow and crackly. Not that he stopped writing. No one did that.

Writing was why my mother took us on a week-long ski trip in Vermont, dropping us off at Killington as the slopes opened and returning to spend long days at a Formica table in a motel room, typing and typing under orders from her writing teacher at the New School. At the end of the day, she was downright thrilled to see us, to start in on our mundane social interactions, to whip up tuna burgers in the kitchenette. All this was so much better than writing, it almost made her giddy.

But these were grown-ups. My theory of writing was: *Go ahead. Why not?* Vroom was on my side. She didn't even mind if I crossed into other arts. You could build shaky bookshelves in shop class, and that was furniture. You could cover a piece of paper with aluminum foil and scribble all over it, and that was art. You could make yourself a vaguely oriental costume out of costume jewelry and your mother's old spring coat, and that was couture.

Jenny, my cousin Lisa, and I got ukuleles, which made us instant musicians, playing mostly three-chord surf music. *Took my Cobra down to the track / hooked to the back of my Cadillac / everyone there was just a-waitin' for me / there were plenty of Stingrays and XKEs* . . . What was an XKE? Who cared?

Until Dad said, "Don't you ever play serious music?"

"Wipeout" was fun, but my father's family worshiped serious music. You had to give it focus, practice, and respect. It was beautiful and demanding, and you had to watch it every second. If you didn't, it would mess with your stomach.

Kids preparing to go on stage at piano recitals sometimes threw up. I never thought it was strange—I felt like throwing up whenever my grandmother asked me to play for her. She, I guess, felt like throwing up whenever she contemplated playing for anyone else. "She had the worst case of stage fright in the recorded history of the known universe," my cousin Lisa says. Every Saturday, for years, I went to music school, and sometimes I still wake up on Saturdays with an uneasy flip in my gut, thinking, *Music. Oh God.*

I began piano lessons at six after it was determined, I don't know by whom, that I had enough talent. I grew up thinking talent was something that could be assessed, in minutes, by an adult with a Russian accent. You could practice your ass off and devote your life to your instrument, but if you had no talent, why bother?

My teacher was a quiet man with a German last name and a steel plate embedded in his forehead, which I tried not to notice. I had a feeling it was somehow related to World War II. All I knew about Mr. Mosbacher was that he was in awe of my family. The lessons were very serious. Practice time—one hour, six evenings a week—was nonnegotiable.

On Saturday mornings, I studied music theory and a kind of complex sight singing at the Chatham Square Music School, a school founded by my grandfather to provide a completely free musical education to talented kids from the Lower East Side. My cousin Lisa and I were the only students there who didn't think of Saturday morning classes as an unheard-of mitzvah and the beginning of a serious adult career. They came to school in dress-up clothes, comb tracks in their hair. This was part of the professionalism they had come to learn. I was several years younger than anyone else in my class, clueless, wearing jeans and cowboy boots, and I usually had no idea what I was supposed to do.

Our teacher, Mr. Martin, would play a melody on the piano, and we would transcribe it onto staff paper. Sometimes I wrote down the correct assortment of notes, but I never understood how. It went on that way for two hours. I was scared of Mr. Martin, wrong notes, and the music school itself, with its quiet hallways and smell of old piano innards. I had to be careful not to blow it, even though I didn't know what *it* was. At ten, I was too old to become a virtuoso. I was clearly being raised as an allaround girl who practiced the piano one hour a day instead of seven. So what was riding on me? How good did I have to be, and for whom?

But I didn't hate music itself. On a good day, I got lost in scales and arpeggios, and my hour passed in a trance. Lying under my grandmother's Steinway as she played Chopin études could just about be a religious experience. The adults said, "Someday you'll thank us for these piano lessons," and the truth is, I do. But I hated what music did to my stomach. Over the years, I've perfected the art of stage fright. Shouldn't it stop already?

THE NEXT GOD first appeared as a graven image: a four-hundred-pound woman who sat on the beach in a thin pink housedress. She was solid as an Easter Island statue, looking mysteriously out to sea. She didn't move. She seemed to melt into the sand. Who was she? Why didn't she speak? Was she sad, or all-knowing?

Aunt Cookie had a question for her, too, but it was rhetorical.

"What is she *doing* out here?"

Appalling.

I was beginning to love Aunt Cookie in a way I never felt for any other relative, but at this moment she made me very uncomfortable.

"Huge. She's absolutely huge. It's disgusting. How could she let herself go like that?"

Perhaps at one time the four-hundred-pound woman looked like anyone else in the aisles at Waldbaum's supermarket. Perhaps she was a newlywed in a Christmas sweater with a job doing data entry. Then one day, only she knows why, she set her interior gauge to four hundred pounds and started eating? Is that what happened?

No! I knew without having been told that people didn't make conscious decisions to become morbidly obese. They didn't set out to be shamed or ashamed. It was never their plan to appear in a public place in order to horrify Aunt Cookie. The four-hundred-pound woman wasn't that calculating. Instead, she was barging slowly through life, hauling her huge body wherever it had to go.

"Well, don't you ever let it happen to you," Aunt Cookie said. And at that moment, it became a possibility. That possibility, and its many permutations, had a name.

Oblivia. She who must be stuffed. I was still in grade school when she nailed me. I fell into a kind of food puberty. Food had always been all around me, but suddenly I was aware, and I was turned on.

I had romantic secret trysts with drugstore chocolate and loving forages through the refrigerator after school—but quietly, so my stepdad wouldn't hear a single clink. On the way home from school, Jenny and I would stand in front of a bakery, looking pitifully through its plate glass window until someone came out and gave us each a cookie, even though our mother said not to.

She didn't believe in dessert, not for girls, anyway, and our father was more interested in expensive cuts of meat than in bakery items. But other people's parents put bowls of nuts and candy around on tables. You could eat them whenever you wanted, and as a result no one ever did but me.

AND NOW THE demigods and other forces began to take turns, entering and exiting as quickly as players in a vaudeville review.

At twelve, I quit piano lessons in order to grow my fingernails long for the first time. Surprisingly, no one in the family tried to stop me, and maybe that's why, after only a month, I found my own teacher and started to play again. Maybe our Samuel was right—maybe music really *was* in my blood. By then, I was old enough to have read my grandfather's books, and I knew more about him. He came from Vitebsk, a town that hopped back and forth between Russia, Lithuania, and Poland as the borders changed. His father was a small-time rabbi known for his ability to discipline boys who refused to pay attention in Hebrew school. His mother was the daughter of Shnayer Tresskanov, a much more learned and mystical rabbi who was consulted by Jews miles from his own shtetl.

The family moved to the Lower East Side of New York in 1895, when Chotzie was six. The second youngest child, he was allowed the luxury of an American public school education instead of a series of sweatshop jobs. Music captured his imagination. He learned piano, hung out at Katz's Music Store with other teenage musicians, snuck into symphony concerts, stole money from his father to buy sheet music, played in jazz combos at Catskill resorts, and paid off his first grand piano in tiny monthly installments. His mother had to travel uptown by subway to Carnegie Hall to see his first performance there, on a Saturday afternoon. The chapter in my grandfather's autobiography that describes it is called "My Mother Rides on the Sabbath." She never told her rabbi husband about it.

At seventeen, Chotzie was able to support his parents by giving piano lessons and teaching English to new immigrants. A few years later, he was hired as piano accompanist for Efrem Zimbalist, a young Russian violinist on his first U.S. tour. Eventually, he did the same thing for my great-uncle Jascha. Uncle Jascha had been a child prodigy in Russia and had come to the United States with his entire extended family, all made homeless by the Russian Revolution. It's worth noting that the Heifetzes—and an astounding number of the other Russian whiz kids—were Jewish.

Chotzie had a bar mitzvah, but it took up only a few pages of his book. He'd chosen music and art over his father's Orthodox Judaism, and it hadn't been much of a contest. My father didn't grow up in a religious home. From the stories he told, I thought of the whole gang as Russians who spoke the language, drank vodka, ate caviar, dressed up in peasant costumes, and read *Anna Karenina* every year in the original. My grandmother knew Yiddish words just like everyone else, but her accent was Russian, and it was Russian she encouraged us to learn. They were their own sort of royalty, anointed by each other.

Chotzie had fallen in love with Jascha's sister Pauline, but she waited seven years before agreeing to marry him. She was beautiful enough to appear in chorus lines and a spread in *Vogue*, capricious enough to pit several boyfriends against each other, and a wonderful pianist who never played in public. She was thirteen years younger than Chotzie, who was prematurely bald and not particularly exotic looking.

The newly created Chotzinoff family moved in with the extended Heifetz family, and my father grew up under the care of a German nurse in a brownstone on West 85th Street. At three, he was introduced to the violin, which he still plays, but he was too rebellious to be molded into a prodigy, and, the story goes, smashed his perfect little violin over his grandfather's head.

In the family compound, rules evolved for music and musicianship, what books to read, and certainly what to eat. For some reason even he couldn't explain, Chotzie wouldn't eat pork unless it was bacon. When my grandmother served him a pork roast, she called it "breast of veal." Rigid standards also held true for things like jigsaw puzzle manufacturers, the engravings of coy shepherdesses that hung on the walls, and the way things looked—the shelves with complete sets of Turgenev and Tolstoy, the little skirted dressing tables scattered with atomizers and tiny photos in tiny frames.

It was important to stay eccentric (but never to be pompous), to play convoluted tricks on each other, to gamble (not for money but for chunks of time). Dad said my grandmother won an hour from her friend Dickie Manson and ordered him to make her a sandwich. She didn't say what kind. In the kitchen at the other end of the house, Dickie piled sardines, marshmallows, mustard, and raw scallops between two pieces of bread.

"Now eat it," my grandmother said, without ever having seen the sandwich.

"All those Jaschas and Mashas and Smashas," Dad's boyhood friend Sam remembers. "They were funny as hell, and they read everything. They kind of liked making everyone on the outside feel stupid."

"My father had to be right about everything," Dad told me. "And it wasn't just important stuff, like music. One day my parents were driving from the city to their house in Ridgefield, and Cookie and I were sitting in the backseat. It was a hot, humid, miserable day. As we drove over the George Washington Bridge, the temperature went down by about ten degrees, and I said, 'It's cool over a body of water!' They all said yes it was. On the way back into the city Sunday night, he said it again, and we all repeated it, one by one, for fun. It's cool over a body of water. And it became kind of a tradition. Everyone in the car always said it, going over the George Washington Bridge.

"But one day I didn't feel like it. I was pissed off about something. We got to the middle of the bridge, and everyone said it but me. And my father pulled the car over to the side and sat there. And I didn't say it. And we sat and sat there for almost an hour until I got out of the car and started walking back to the city. Stubborn. That's how we were."

On the other hand, this was New York in the 1930s, and Dad soon learned about life beyond Heifetzes. He tells me he went wherever he wanted—deep into Central Park in the middle of the night; to the World's Fair by subway, where he swears he stayed for several days, enjoying the possibility that everyone was worried sick about him at home.

The Russian musician gang had thinned out somewhat by the time I came along, but it still had its traditions. No bedtime for kids, for instance, and no set meal time for anyone. If you felt like a beefsteak tomato sandwich on the thinnest toast at 4:00 P.M., fine. If you happened to catch two dozen crabs by moonlight, it would make sense to boil them up at midnight. Everyone but me could taste the difference between regular pepper and something called Tellicherry pepper. Regular pepper would do only in a pinch.

My father told me some of it was just plain wrong. He, for instance, liked to eat steaks so expensive they *better* be good; they, my grandmother and Aunt Cookie, lived for cheap, sinewy cuts of meat, marrow bones, and the little triangular flap that hung over a chicken's rear. (My father, using dubious Yiddish, called it the *pupik.*)

At twelve, I was old enough to participate in New Year's Eve. We played charades, only it was called "The Game" and men always played against women. It was fun if you knew a lot of obscure quotes, or wanted to, or had grown up this way and didn't know any different. Visiting adults were sometimes horrified because if you didn't know Shakespeare sonnets inside and out, The Game was less than welcoming. My mother hated it. I liked it, unless I screwed up. It was a good place to visit but you wouldn't want to live there.

At fifteen, my father's family was only one of the things I wanted to leave behind.

I thought leaving might be every bit as exhilarating as writing.

I TALKED MY mother into sending me to boarding school at Phillips Academy in Andover, Massachusetts. I brought my beloved suitcase-style record player and a whole box of LPs. After listening to the Allman Brothers and Traffic obsessively, I realized

I could sit at the piano in the basement of my dorm and write a song. And if you looked at the back of an album long enough, you became aware of obscure songwriters. The Rolling Stones did "Love in Vain," but Robert Johnson wrote it. I finally found a Robert Johnson record, and then more original blues musicians: Howlin' Wolf, Muddy Waters, Lightnin' Hopkins—and after that, no limit. Roosevelt Sykes, an old guy from Helena, Arkansas, illuminated piano boogie and blues. I was terrible, but I played all the time, trying to get my left hand to break free of Mr. Mosbacher and move closer to the Mississippi Delta, the birthplace of *my* idea of serious music.

Once again I found myself in church, looking at a plaster statue of Jesus, even though I had a pretty good background as a sinner by then. In tenth grade, I had a captain-of-the-football-team boyfriend. His mother still mailed him clean laundry every week and he still went to Catholic church. I went to mass with him a few times, dressed up in a skirt, my legs freezing in the Massachusetts wind, and we stopped for donuts on the way.

Eating junk food in front of him felt much more intimate than the sex we'd had the night before. Until a few weeks ago, he'd been a virgin. I hadn't. Sex was just something I did early and defiantly, even though I was a good girl still working hard to earn the gold star on the term paper. It was just another facet of my unusual and fascinating personality, I thought, as I sneaked to my boyfriend's room after curfew, never getting busted. Yet walking to church with a boy who believed in God made me feel exposed. It seemed to have something to do with all that powdered sugar on my mouth.

He walked to the rail for communion, the most promising athlete/scholar on campus, built like a Greek god but wearing red polyester bell-bottoms. He whispered a prayer to himself as he returned. I tried to say something irreverent—wasn't that the point of me?—and he frowned. So I looked up, and there was Jesus again, still looking sad and confused. All this *mishegass* had erupted in the years since he'd been born, and yet all he'd wanted was to teach people to love each other.

Love mankind, be a pacifist, be like Martin Luther King Jr. and Mahatma Ghandi? Move toward love and away from sin? I drew a blank. I hadn't taken those courses. Besides, sin was how I had fun. The adults in my life appeared to be swingin' adulterers, and boarding school was just prep for that life, adolescence just a formality. We ran our own lives, lived and moved in semi-sophisticated herds, saw our parents on vacations. This was a time and place when a young male professor who slept with a high-school girl and didn't get fired for it was considered a romantic hero, and the girl unbelievably cool. Once, while home on Christmas break, I got wasted on gin and tonics at a party and tried to sneak down the hall into bed without running into my mother, but there she was. She asked me what happened. I didn't lie. The next morning she sat me down for a bit of advice. Gin and tonics, she said, are awfully high in calories. White wine is always a better choice.

Only once in a while did she mention that some of her relatives couldn't control their Oblivias. Wasn't there an elderly cousin who loved drinking so much that even when they took his clothes away he went out on Park Avenue naked, hoping to make it to a liquor store and back before someone caught him? Had I heard it was heroin, not gin? What about that great-aunt whose hired female "companion" complained she was "up to a quart a day?"

My mother thought drinks improved most situations, and she looked forward to the hour at which it was permissible to have a few, but she also married her first two Jewish men because they were thought unlikely to become drunks. My father, not the kind of Jew she thought he was, drank over-the-counter cough syrup, and later, when that became prescription-only, vodka.

I thought drinks were silly because smoking pot was more fashionable, and everyone had started doing it in ninth or tenth grade. I loved the ritual. You had to get close to each other to share a joint, you had to lean against alluring flannel-shirted teenage boys. Dope was a reason to stay out late talking about nothing and laughing about everything. You got to pass through the living room in an altered state, spending just enough time with your parents—their brandy and Benedictine, Frank Sinatra lifestyle—to make fun of them later. They flirted with each other, even though they were married and old.

We had a better grasp of fun. We invented hilarious games: cram as many whole grapes into your mouth as possible without breaking the skin and then *whoosh,* have them shoot out as you started to laugh uncontrollably. Finally understand why a guitarist would play a fifteen-minute solo. Get the munchies and eat with impunity! Pass those Pepperidge Farm goldfish and be quick about it! Wasted, I could see myself as not fat, but the brazen custodian of a large, unwieldy body, not to mention large, unwieldy appetites. For this, I even got respect.

"You have to eat like a horse to be you," said one of those skinny prep school girls, jeans hanging gracefully from her hip-bones. "I mean, I kind of admire it. Did you ever watch a horse eat? It's hard."

"Semiprofound," I said, or something like that. "Yeah, I'm just . . . yeah, horse."

Wanting to buy some pot made it completely legit to walk up to a particularly handsome boy to ask if he knew where I could get some.

"I just happen to have a lid right here," he said, patting the breast pocket of his tweed blazer. Voilà. He had to get close to me to smoke that joint up in the woods outside my dorm. I remember the way his lips looked, exactly.

Most of the people I knew at prep school drank openly. It wasn't strictly legal, but it couldn't have been wrong, either, because if it were, why would your parents set a wine glass at your spot when you came home from vacation? People's fathers drank cocktails from a can on the sidelines at football games. Getting a keg and drinking it on school property must have been frowned upon, but I have no proof because it was so easy to get drunk. I just wasn't very good at it. I lay on my dorm bed and watched the room spin and considered throwing up. I had no inhibitions then, and it didn't help me any. I thought it would be somehow noble to get drunk and blurt things out.

I ached to blurt the story of this Jewish guy, my editor at the school newspaper. His Jewishness wouldn't have registered with me if he hadn't brought it up, but his family went to Israel over winter break, and he was witty and self-deprecating and not entirely gorgeous or desirable, the way I understood a classic WASP boyfriend to be. I wasn't entirely gorgeous or desirable to him, either. Nothing like the real *shikses* for whom he strove so transparently, in his East Coast Jewish guy way.

Once a week, we were allowed to stay up all night to lay out the paper. He called me "Chotzinoff" and raved about *The Brothers Karamazov*, baiting me into an endless sarcasm contest. Insulting each other, we talked so fast no one else bothered to try to understand us. The one thing he didn't seem to find ironic was his Judaism. I didn't know why, and I wouldn't have asked because religion embarrassed me, and I didn't want to think about why a smart boy would believe in bullshit. Luckily, he also talked about Elie Wiesel, which steered the whole Jewish thing toward the Holocaust, a fascinating and disturbing subject that I thought had nothing to do with God. From there, the conversation possibilities were endless. Talking was a brand new thing to do with a boy. (I compared it to the one real date I'd been on in my life— stilted conversation over New England boiled dinner. Oy.)

Jewish Editor Boy began to mess with my hormones, flooding me with visions of being his real, live girlfriend or his coeditor or the person who riffed in public with him on the campus radio station. I had certainly had crushes before, but usually on people understood to be crush-worthy because they were handsome, popular, athletic, or just the best specimen in a limited group. A wiseass Jewish guy was different. Other females didn't seem aware of him until the strength of my adoration made him magically attractive, and suddenly there was competition. And so, though I wanted him in a lot of ways, I was eligible only for one. During those many sleepless nights, I had sex with him whenever I could. Being so much better than nothing, it was painfully good. Addictive, in its way, like other things.

SEX AND DRUGS were fine in public, but I practiced my main jones by myself. While babysitting, I discovered Betty Crocker icing in a can. I ate all the cookies in the package but one, as if they wouldn't know who did it. I finished the grilled cheese crusts on the children's plates. I ate their Halloween, Valentine's, and birthday candy. The first time I attempted to bake my own birthday cake, I ate so much batter there was nothing left but a cupcake's worth, and I threw that out. In retrospect, I don't know why I told my mother, who was tall and thin and elegant. At five foot seven and 140 pounds, I had long since passed her on my way up the scale. I was merely curvaceous, but that could lead quickly to fat. I was surprised to learn that I reminded her of herself.

"When I lived alone in the Village," she said, "I'd have a butterscotch sundae at a drugstore, and then I'd walk a few blocks to the next drugstore and have another." She said this while slipping into her size 4 pants from Jax and hoping I would accept her weakness as a cautionary tale. *Don't let this happen to you.* Just to make sure I understood how serious this too-much-food stuff could be, she turned my birthday cake story into a cocktail-hour anecdote, and then everyone heard, and no one knew what to say.

The situation escalated. My mother clipped diets out of magazines and put them where I'd "accidentally" see them, bought me big dresses designed for camouflage, and took herself to seminars on calm acceptance. I found a note on her bedside table: "I will try to love Robin, I will try to love her because she is overweight, I will try . . ." If my body were different, she wouldn't have to try. But if I transformed myself, she would shower me with love. Meanwhile, I would try to love myself. I would try. But when things got really hairy, I pretended I didn't even know myself.

Step one was eating your own birthday cake before it went into the oven. Step two was the four-hundred-pound woman on the beach.

I wasn't at step two yet, though. I tried Dr. Stillman's Quick Teen Diet, the original hardboiled-egg-and-cottage-cheese regime. I'd be giddy with starvation and a sense of impending thinness. A week or so later, I'd be stoned with my primitive goddess again, feeling as good as I'd ever felt. But then it would be time for a sacrifice. Oblivia wanted the whitest goat, the purest virgin, the 95-pound anorexic girl with the glowing face, the size 4, 2, 0. When it turned out I was none of these, she was disgusted and I felt very bad, very lonely. Eventually, I would eat something, assuming it would make me feel better, and it did. But then *wham!*

Food was the mother of all vengeful gods. When I got interested in pirates, of all things, I thought of it immediately. You wouldn't have wanted to get mixed up with seventeenth-century pirates—the guys like Calico Jack Rackham who gave their boats sardonic names like *Happy Adventure* and *The Black Joke*. The more destructive the joke turned out to be, the harder they laughed, and they seldom released a prisoner.

People said things like, "Just a small piece for me, it's awfully rich." Rich, ha. Rich was what made things taste good. I ate sugar out of the bowl.

I TRIED TO obliterate Oblivia with talk. It was easy to believe in talk. Sooner or later, everyone I knew "saw someone" to "talk things over." This someone might have started out as a Freudian analyst, morphed over the years into a psychiatrist who gave a little more than "I see, and how did *that* make you feel?" and then became the sliding-scale social worker of our no money years, or even a feminist peer counselor. In the beginning, this person didn't know you, didn't have any expertise in your big issue— your wife who left, your eating disorder, your teen daughter who slashes her wrists when she wants attention. I was raised to think that when trouble threatens, you go see someone.

Before I was born, my mother went to her analyst four mornings a week. When she left my father, he gave it a shot too. He thought he could rebuild a bond with my mother by unzipping his psyche the way she had. He talked to the "goddamn head-shrinker," but my mom never came back, so that was the end of that. Meanwhile, my stepfather teamed up with one therapist after another, distilling their latest findings for publication in glossy magazines. There was a guy whose expertise was the giving and getting of criticism. There were the marriage experts—quite a few married to each other.

I mention this not to mock it, but to clear up the semantics. No, we didn't go to church or synagogue or Quaker meeting, and we didn't understand the mystery of therapy, but we agreed to wait until the moment it was revealed, and to learn its language, using words like "depressed" and "nervous breakdown." "Depressed" didn't sound like much of a kick, but I was intrigued by "breakdown." It sounded romantic. At a Gothically beautiful country home for crazy people, I could write poetry and lose weight.

A more modern kind of breakdown was the drug-inspired "freakout." One my friends had one—fueled by one night of LSD and virginity losing—and within days she was gone, sent to Vermont for top-secret mental rehab. I envied her. She got to skip an entire semester of school, and no one knew when she'd be back. Also, the freakout center, unlike our school, was coed. What was *that* like?

In boarding school I contracted a broken heart from my long association with Jewish Editor Boy. My symptom was bottomless, lazy misery. I decided not to leave my room. There was no grown-up around to say, " Oh sweetie, he's just a boy, big deal. Get on with your life," but I did get to go see the school counselor, a wonderful hippy woman who lived off campus and literally let me cry on her shoulder. When my mother came up to school, they talked about me, about my "issues," which pissed me off yet gave me a warm, protected feeling all the same. My mother was doing her best to take care of me—to have me see that if I understood myself and where I'd come from, I would feel better and act better.

But no one knew when that sort of thing would actually happen. So for at least ten more years my sister and I bled my mother's bank account for hours and hours of talking to someone.

At several points, my mother was paying someone to help me come to mean conclusions about my mother and I don't know how she stood it.

My first writing teacher at Andover was Hart Leavitt, on the verge of retirement and still playing regular saxophone gigs with a big band. He had written a textbook called *Stop, Look, and Write!* You looked at a picture, you wrote. You looked at those pictures intently. Your eyes hurt! Mr. Leavitt taught me to think small and specific, which was handy because I couldn't seem to care about big social statements or the ins and outs of humankind. I learned to laugh at essays that concluded with "thus we see." I tried to adopt everything about him, even his handwriting. When I edit my own stuff now, I see the no-nonsense scribbles of Mr. Leavitt, or at least I hope I do.

Fat Jack Zucker, poetry professor, was an utter non-WASP from the Bronx with a thick accent that filled his poetry recitations with whiney splendor. He was unkempt. He convened his class over Dunkin' Donuts in his own unkempt living room. He knew all kinds of Real Poets—I still see their bylines in the *New Yorker*—and they came to our class and critiqued our self-referential verse. When I read anything poetic to myself, I do it in Fat Jack's accent.

I think I was a good student. I got published in school newspapers and literary magazines. I probably could have graduated from a good college and perhaps become an English teacher, eventually publishing a piece of fiction. Wasn't that the blueprint for a writing career?

Maybe, but toward the end of my junior year a pamphlet from the United States Coast Guard appeared in my Andover

mailbox. I'd never considered joining the armed forces but as-
sumed it would be pretty much like running off with a circus.
Plus, there'd be plenty to write about. No more sitting around a
large oak table reading and critiquing short stories about high
school seniors sitting around a large oak table sharing angst. I
tacked the letter up on the wall next to my single bed and
watched fantasies pop into my head the way they used to when
I was writing but not working at writing. Vroom was definitely
involved. Also, I loved the way the letter was addressed to "Mr.
Robin Chotzinoff."

My father had gone into the Air Force, had never attended
college, and didn't seem to care whether I did or not. But he
couldn't see me in the armed forces. "Do you realize they'll tell
you what to do every fucking second?" he said. "When to eat,
what to wear, what to say? You wouldn't last a week."

He was right. Even I knew that. But by then, to continue on as
planned would have been dull. That spring I managed to gradu-
ate one year early from high school because this would accelerate
the arrival of the excitement I knew was about to happen.

Obviously, I was going to have to go to college—what else did
you do after high school, other than join the Coast Guard?—so I
scrambled around and got admitted to Bryn Mawr College in
mainline Pennsylvania. By the next fall, I was a freshman in a
place that was perfect for scholarly young women who wanted to
be left alone to study ancient Greece or cultural anthropology.
Which I wasn't.

Over the summer, I had reinvented myself. I now played an
old black guitar with green palm trees painted on it. I wrote songs

of misery and ennui and was starting to like the idea of singing them in public.

I smoked pot, cut class, and stared out the window of my neo-Gothic dormitory, which prided itself on being full of virgins. My boyfriend was the most shocking partner available in that time and place. He rode around campus on a green plastic skateboard, grew Spanish moss from the ceiling of his dorm room, distilled his own rotgut booze from cafeteria fruit punch, and introduced me to the exotic sport of hiking. We drove to New Orleans over spring break and camped among the live oaks. In the French Quarter, I saw the silhouette of a woman slowly taking off her clothes. I wasn't even sure what I was studying anymore.

My first tab of acid was a little shred of white paper imprinted with a tiny Mr. Natural. I hesitated.

"I heard you can go crazy," I told my boyfriend.

"What do you mean, 'crazy'?"

"Like, you can go on a trip and never come back."

"Oh, like Art Linkletter's daughter. She thought she could fly, man, and she jumped off a building?"

"Yeah," I said, a little embarrassed. "Like that."

"That's a myth. Some people think acid messes with your immune system a little, but that's all. You may get a cold or something. You really shouldn't do it if you don't want to."

But of course I did. The high came on gradually and was like nothing I'd ever experienced. I continued tripping for the next ten years, and I still can't describe what happened. I would read Aldous Huxley, thinking maybe he could do a better job—those who go through the "door in the wall" never really come back, and stuff like that—but the big revelations were confined to the actual tripping hours. Sometimes I wrote myself notes, trying to remember. Almost always, I wrote the words "freight elevator. Door opens between floors!"

Colors intensified—sunsets like stained glass windows—and sex could be absorbing, not to mention long lasting, provided I could get a boy interested, except that boys on acid trips had an unfortunate tendency to get all wrapped up in pointless things, like a pinecone or a Hot Wheels car.

The future was about to kick in. I just knew it.

It turned out to be so predictable. At the college bookstore one day I purchased a bag of Chips Ahoy! cookies and a copy of *On the Road* and devoured them both in one afternoon. After that, what to do was clear. *Go. Be gone. Begone!* Again, I knew what to do with my composition notebook—take it on a symbolic hitch-hiking trip to a summer job interview in Lancaster. I was picked up by an Amish man driving a Dodge Dart, his legs covered by a threadbare handmade quilt. Then an honest-to-God long-haul trucker! Both men had regional accents so thick I could barely understand them, but so what? I didn't get the job but, again, so what? Freedom was the point, even though I took the train back from Lancaster, instead of hitchhiking, so as to have more unin-terrupted time for journal writing.

I was figuring things out so fast I could barely write quickly enough. People made everything so complicated—the grades, the family, the career plans—when all you really had to do was just keep moving, watching as various humble objects along the high-way became sort of holy. Pieces of pie, names of towns, fluttering garbage. It was all so much more important than the remote concepts I was raised on. Things! Motion! Altered states!

It must have been horrible when I held forth at the college cafeteria. I was horrible at least half the time—cheating on my boyfriend out of sheer eroding conscience. I forced him to dump me.

Since I didn't get the Lancaster summer job, I stayed at Bryn Mawr and worked on the landscaping crew, a blue-collar job I thought would make me strong and lean and Gary Snyder–like—living alone, drinking green tea, and immersing myself in as much wilderness as suburban Pennsylvania had to offer.

Instead, I ate. In a month, I gained twenty-five pounds. Isolation turned out to be horrible. I couldn't drive, didn't have a bike, was marooned at home. I wrote not a word. Sometimes inspiration would hit me while I was weeding between brick pavers or ripping Virginia creeper out of the juniper bushes, but when I got home at night there was this matter of muscle and endurance. You had to sit and write for no one. You had to sit with yourself, confronting the deep, embarrassing neediness. Under a barrage of books and sugar, I could make that feeling retreat until I felt almost nothing, but that didn't make me happy either.

This might have been a reasonable time to make the connection between higher education and how interesting your jobs and circumstances get to be without one. Or I could have toughed out a dismal situation, because I'd heard everyone had to do that sooner or later.

Instead, I called my mother and begged for money. I told her I needed to go to Boulder, Colorado, to Naropa Institute, where I intended to become a Tibetan Buddhist. Buddhism didn't count as religion—it was more a mental discipline—so I'd certainly be safe from God-fearing weirdos. Also, I could study writing with Allen Ginsberg and Robert Creeley and all the Beat greats, at the brand new Jack Kerouac School of Disembodied Poetics.

What else could she do with me? She sent a check.

Meanwhile, I spent one last weekend with Dad back at the Hampton Boat Works. I had a new half sister: Marina, whose childhood was being spent in a marina. She toddled around in a diaper and white T-shirt, and we were interested in each other. The adults, however, irritated me until I got blisters on my tongue from biting it. I wanted my father to grasp the momentousness of me on my way west, about to start a new life. Instead, he found the Naropa catalog hilarious. A special seminar was to be taught by a visiting monk named Wang Chuck. Wang Chuck! What a load of horseshit!

"How about some dinner, there, Wangchuk?" he asked me. "Can you give me a hand with this wiring, Wangchuck? Why the long face, Wangchuck?"

Obviously, my father's mind was not yet open enough to learn the lessons of Wang Chuck, maybe never would be. Philistines. I was surrounded by them.

I went to Boulder on the Grey Rabbit, a bus lined with foam mattresses where the seats would usually be—very Merry Prankster. The trip was awful. All forty of us slept spooned, uncomfortably close. I traveled light, stuffing my guitar case with an extra pair of underpants, an alternate T-shirt, a toothbrush, pens, notebooks, and an actual guitar. As much as I wanted to be free,

free, free, I felt intensely self-conscious. How could I sleep without squashing the tiny Hispanic man on my left? How could I stand the hair-spray smell of the red-headed woman on my right? When were we going to eat? Did I look genuinely Beat, or did people think I was just a poser college girl? Did they think about me at all?

I got horny and romantic in waves. One second I wanted to jump the bones of the relief driver, who sat in the rear of the bus getting high all day, waiting for his shift. I wanted to feel his long blond hair pouring over my shoulders—I doubt I even looked at his face. And then I'd want a real boyfriend, someone to move in with, someone to eat dinner with, someone to own books with and dance with, someone to play my songs for, handsome but still sweet and understanding. I cast my eyes over every man on that bus, but couldn't kid myself.

As we passed from Kansas into Colorado, the land began to undulate, brown and nosebleed dry, the sky high and cloudless. I sat still and waited for a portentous feeling, something along the lines of *here you are, and here you will write great things.* So far, so good.

In Boulder, I met a woman who had hitchhiked down from Montana wearing a tie-dyed shirt and cutoffs so short you could see her pubic hair. We went out for macrobiotic stir-fry and she flinched when the waitress handed her a fork.

"Chopsticks, *please,*" she said. "I never put metal in my mouth."

I lived in a sorority house with other members of my meditation group. My roommate was sixteen—another spoiled kid from the New York suburbs. We meditated for three hours every day—

watched our breath, let extraneous thoughts go. The room where we sat was sunny, with shining wooden floors and always a small vase of flowers, a sort of altar.

We sat there, and that was that. We weren't untangling complex theology or any theology at all. The minute the gong rang to begin the meditation, my brain flooded with what could only be called sins. All the promises I didn't keep. I came in search of inner peace, whatever that was, but instead I wanted to jump out of my own skin. I was hungry all the time.

Meals were at a frat house cafeteria. On the first day, a woman there handed me a card that read: "I choose not to speak today." Within five minutes, several people told me that they were voluntarily celibate. I met people who followed different eastern swamis, who wore patchouli and prayer beads! I met the fiftyish wife of a career Navy man who had run away to Boulder to find *her* inner self, dressing every day in rainbow silk robes, her hair in a stiffly sprayed pageboy. I met many musicians, all disciples of a free-ranging jazz I tried over and over again to grasp, but couldn't. (I stuck with three chords.)

A chorus girl from Las Vegas had saved all her money to come to Naropa for just one summer to pursue her calling as a "contemplative psychiatrist." Her white clothes complemented her butt-length dark red hair. She was six feet tall without the platform shoes she always wore, with maroon lipstick as slick and reflective as the surface of a Jell-O mold. It went without saying that all the men in Boulder preferred their women all-natural, with armpit hair and perhaps little strings of bells around their waists, but the chorus girl did not go unnoticed by the unbleached-muslin boys. She sat up late at night playing Risk with them, but never wanted to fool around.

One night in her dorm room, while listening to Joni Mitchell and drinking straight vodka out of Dixie Cups, she began kissing me with those sticky lips. I bolted and spent some time walking around drunk in a graveyard, wondering if this could be some kind of turning point. A good one? A bad one? Then I went to 7–Eleven because that's what I always did.

No one had written edgy, outsider fiction about binge eating. I never threw on my leather jacket and told my friends, "Yo, I'm going to hitchhike to Safeway and buy the giant box of Ritz crackers and a liter of real Coke and a frozen carrot cake and go get straight, man. Don't wait up!"

In fact, I never told anyone. My food jones ran in the background, like an outdated computer program.

Chogyam Trungpa Rimpoche, spiritual leader of the Buddhist college, occasionally made an appearance. Our teachers prepared by setting up a throne on a raised platform, surrounding it with gold Buddhas, flowers, and incense. Trungpa would sit there, smiling sarcastically at us, holding a can of beer. Nothing radiated from him that I could see. I was no Buddhist, even though I wrote my mother letters hinting at a spiritual awakening that had set me on a reassuring path. In fact, lots of people were walking that path at Naropa, but I didn't see how. Sitting still on a little cushion, worshiping at the feet of a Tibetan drunk, drinking a lot and dancing to the clamor of other students whaling on cardboard boxes with wooden spoons—that was the Naropa school band, and anyone could be in it—or holding arcane Hindu poses for long minutes until your muscles screamed and tears rolled down your face—how could any of this open the door to anything?

I decided that because I wasn't the spiritual type I'd be disillusioned. That would be my new persona. I would blow all my money at the bar at the Hotel Boulderado. Of course, I could still be a writer. A lot of writers were disillusioned.

My teacher was William Burroughs. I was the only girl in his class, and Burroughs seemed to have an aversion to girls. It didn't matter if I handed in any work because he never read it. In class, we'd write "automatically" for five minutes or so, and then cut up our pages and paste them back together in a more pleasingly random order.

Allen Ginsberg, visiting professor, didn't seem to like girls either. Robert Creeley, whose spare and lovelorn poetry had captured me back in boarding school, turned out to be obsessed with UFOs and haunted houses. It was all he would talk about.

People at Naropa came off like mystics. Their message went something like this: If, while playing cat's cradle, you stare at the tangled strings intently, you will suddenly see the Eiffel Tower. According to them, the only way to see God was through revelation. Unfair! Why did the pubic-hair-showing Montana girl get to experience Enlightenment, while all I got was another ten pounds? Sorry, but I only saw tangled string.

Back from Naropa, living alone in my dad's New York apartment, I still had a little summer left—just enough time to have that breakdown I'd been planning. After a short phone call to a Bryn Mawr psychiatrist, I was put on Stelazine, an early antidepressant. It was very Grimm Brothers. A stooped old crone whose wall was covered with diplomas gave me a bottle filled with magic pills. "Be careful with these," she said. "Go home before taking your first dose. Don't operate heavy machinery."

The magic pills turned me into a frog sitting on a log, not moving, occasionally letting out a croak. The nasty inner chatter continued in my head, but I couldn't move from the log, even when it rained or when lightning struck. I was just so tired. I threw the pills out and never saw that old witch again. Besides, it was time to go back to college.

I don't remember much about that final semester of classes, only the one performance I got to play at the College Inn with a band called Fats Chance and his Blues Marauders. Maybe I could turn out like Marcia Ball or Bonnie Raitt. I wanted to sing the truth about things, particularly men, although I'd never really gotten to know one for very long.

But the best song I wrote had nothing to do with love. It was a hymn to Vroom. I had a brand new Epiphone bluegrass guitar, wide and curvaceous and blonde, and it inspired me to write what I thought was just brilliant:

I sold my soul to United Parcels and I stood out on the side of the road
All I had was a pocketful of independence
I never carried a lighter load . . .

And then I really did get to go. My grandmother, the Heifetz sister, had died during the summer and left me five thousand dollars, and no one could stop me.

IN 1976, FIVE thousand dollars was enough to live on for nearly a year, so I went to San Francisco to look for work and audition for bands—a self-conscious project if there ever was one. I signed up with the city job office and read the bulletin board at the guitar shop, but that was as far as it went.

I look back at myself thinking, *Good Lord, why didn't she get off her ass? Learn ballroom dancing! Go to the Sex Museum! Feed the homeless!*

At least I had a social life—when you bought drugs, you met people. Alone, I ate steadily until finally I grew as fat as my mother always feared I would. Or I mixed the two hobbies, enjoying a peanut butter sandwich with one or two Quaaludes sprinkled on top. Or I'd snort cocaine from a mirror, just like those idiot disco people, because drugs could make you well—maybe better than well—which was a hotter prospect than waking up, getting dressed, eating a nutritious breakfast, going to work. Better than well was surprisingly dull, but I was too terrified of adult life to notice.

Finally, I took out a U.S. road atlas and put a star on every city where someone I knew lived. I didn't care if I knew them well or practically not at all. I still didn't know how to drive a car, so I signed up with a ride board, offered to pay for gas, and waited.

Rose, in Tucson, was my first stop. I had known her slightly at college, and there she was in Arizona, taking a year off. The point of her existence seemed to be to ride around town on an ancient motorcycle, which was enough to make me rent a room in her house and skip the rest of my American road trip. Late at night, she took me to a gravel parking lot and let me skid around on her bike, falling and stalling and loving it, until I got my license.

We signed up for classes in motorcycle mechanics, taught in a desert bomb shelter by a militia-type guy. I strove to catch some air among the saguaros; to take apart a two-stroke engine; to diagnose a troublesome ping. We called our teacher "Teach," because he liked to instruct us not just about internal combustion but about life itself.

"I know you've seen my wife, Shorty, around here, and I want to explain the way this works," he said. "Shorty and I have an open marriage. It's the only way to go." Then he'd eye the mattresses spread out in the bomb shelter and Rose and I would laugh our asses off.

But he knew engines, and engines tied into my earliest sensations of lift-off and inspiration. Troubleshooting in particular was an elegant process: You got the factory manual, looked up the symptoms, and tried one thing after another until your problem dissolved. Then you felt handy as hell, and the next engine issue was just a little less mysterious.

I knew it wouldn't lead to anything. Rose would go back to college when the summer heat chased everyone away. So I learned to occupy the moment. It wasn't complicated. Rose's motorcycle cleared the garbage from my mind. How could I not feel joy when all I had to do was zoom around, watch the road, feel the red dust and the wind in my face, and stop at Circle K for a $1.99 bottle of Andre Champagne?

Sometimes you had to *just be*—I'd heard that from the Tibetan Buddhists, and could never get the hang of it. But sometimes, when you had no choice but to *just be,* you were also allowed to be amused—to study the cowboys two-stepping at the Oxbow Bar, to wonder why their trucks and belt buckles were so big when they themselves were so bitty. You didn't have to detach from your surroundings. You could be curious instead. We Jews think God gives us just this one life, and if we don't try to enjoy it, he's a little insulted. I didn't know that yet.

I had just turned nineteen.

I SETTLED IN Berkeley, California, and stayed there four years, during which I worked my way through one steady boyfriend and several apartments, and finally ended up living in a garage behind a country/folk songwriter who let me and my electric piano constitute his entire backup band. We played at a bar he called the Broom Closet, and I worked as a street vendor on Telegraph Avenue, selling earrings my boss swore were handcrafted.

If there was a church or a synagogue in Berkeley, it never registered with me. On the other hand, I ate at the Hare Krishna restaurant and had friends who called themselves "spiritual," which had something to do with nature, psilocybin, and expensive moisturizer from the health food store. Spiritual girls didn't stress about anything. They did Tai Chi; everything about them smelled good. They went for walks alone in eucalyptus groves. I wished I could be a spiritual girl instead of a musician who played underground shows at an abandoned supermarket—you got ten hits of nitrous oxide with your admission ticket. But my ambitions interfered. I wanted to play *my* songs instead of Lowell George's and Jerry Garcia's, and I was annoyed that the piano was seen as a rhythm instrument, in the background with the bass and drums. I wanted to perform, and for this I needed an audience. Boys, for instance, who carried my amp home for me after shows.

In general, though, men were a crapshoot. The nice ones were drippy, and I was too skittish for monogamy. The mean ones were mean, of course. After a one-eyed boyfriend who looked like Errol Flynn and lied compulsively—"We have to go see my aunt Tessa—she's about to give me two hundred thousand dollars. I would never do heroin because I think it's wrong. I love you."—I decided it was time for a few standards.

I developed the Dog-and-Jesus Rule. A man had to pass this test: (A) be able to deal with dogs, because if you didn't have any at the moment, you would, and (B) never mention Jesus, because it gave me the creeps. While it was easy to believe that the U.S. government was trying to poison us all by spraying the Mexican marijuana crop with paraquat, it was ludicrous to talk about the son of God. You could trust only an atheist.

In Berkeley, being The Counterculture was a point of pride. We mated with each other, dropped acid with each other, and went down to Mexico every January and February with each other after the Christmas street-vending rush. We constituted our own little cult. There was no need to go to the outside world. We even had a therapist.

Rashi the Tarot Guy practiced from a card table on the side-walk in the afternoon because he devoted his mornings to his mail-order business—he sold used underpants—and the escort clients he culled from two different personal ads. He described himself as "tall, surfer-type blond" and "college guy, well-muscled, brown hair and eyes." In person, Rashi was maybe five foot six, 120 pounds, with long stringy black hair, thick glasses, and acne. But none of his male patrons minded. He put people at ease.

If Rashi said, "Don't worry about money this week—you just won't make any. Work on your music. You won't get laid either," I believed him, and it took the pressure off. He was usually right, too.

I didn't tell him about my battle with the It's-It, a convenience store treat involving two oatmeal cookies dipped in chocolate, with ice cream inside. Most people could eat about half of one, but my tolerance grew and grew. I drove around dropping bits of food on my lap and wondering how to outrun Oblivia, and then I'd return to Telegraph Avenue or the Broom Closet to get high among my people in more acceptable ways.

I might still be in Northern California if it weren't for the Dead Kennedys, who came into being in San Francisco and wiped out any trace of the country rock and blues I was just getting comfortable playing. Musicians I'd known for years were ditching their Peter Frampton hair, getting purple buzz cuts, and buying shiny black suits and skinny ties at the thrift store.

Punk audiences were nasty and unforgiving. They wanted four-minute songs; snotty, theatrical front-men; and something offensive in every set. Half-heartedly, I died white stripes into my hair and appeared on stage in a mechanic's suit wrapped with duct tape. My stage name was Helena Hoseclamp. It didn't fly.

I took my demo tape to New York City to shop myself around. The record company guys told me that although my songs were unusual, I couldn't sing my way out of a paper bag. It didn't seem fair that the world couldn't accept a female songwriter with a lousy voice—after all, so many famous men had that exact qualification.

I WENT TO Denver to visit my father, who had moved there at fifty to start a new life. If he hadn't, his wife would have taken my two-year-old sister, Marina, away from the claustrophobic inertia that permeated their New York apartment.

I didn't *get* Denver. It had no counterculture, no espresso places, barely a punk band. In winter, a brown cloud hung over downtown, a neighborhood no one actually lived in. Strangest of all, Dad was writing again, holding forth on classical music in *Denver Magazine,* and hosting a weekly PBS show. In New York, he hadn't left the apartment before dark, and was anything but a serious music expert, at least not compared to all those Jaschas and Mashas and Smashas. But in Denver he lunched with one group of people and had cocktails with another, went to the symphony, hunted ducks, and bought a massive new motorcycle—all in one day. People were impressed. I'd never seen him so content, but I wasn't the kind of person who said things like "I'm so happy for you!"

I thought I'd move to Denver for about a month. It would distract me from my dim prospects as a musician. It would be a relief to quit trying so hard, and no one would stop me from doing some subtle bragging about my sophisticated West Coast days. Besides, logistics were so much easier—apartments were cheap, you never had to walk anywhere or take a bus, and I even contemplated getting a bank loan in order to buy my first new motorcycle.

You don't get a bank loan if you don't have a real job, and you don't get a decent or interesting job if you couldn't last four years in college. At twenty-two, I typed stock certificates in the basement of a bank, waited tables, and shined shoes.

My mother sensed my discouragement. She continued to tell people I was taking a year off from college, even though it had now been five.

My father was more optimistic. You didn't need a formal education, he said, as long as you read books.

"Other than that," he said, "all you need are a few buzz words."

In this case, the words pertained to the oil business. Sam, my dad's childhood friend, had discovered the biggest oil field in Montana and quietly supported him ever since. My father had always thought someone would come along to save him from depressing real jobs in the depressingly real world, and for a while he relaxed in Denver, building his reputation as a writer who could discourse on Tchaikovsky. But then he decided to go into business, to discover his own oil fields. How hard could it be? He printed up stationery and invited me to come in as a partner.

It sounded better than telling strangers about the shrimp special or putting a spit shine on a pair of ostrich cowboy boots at the National Western Stock Show. In the oil business, I figured, I could wear those boots myself. Carry a briefcase. "Visit with people," as they said in Colorado. I was starting to think about writing things down again, and the small towns where oil was being found were full of people who lived in places so unlike Manhattan as to be utterly fascinating.

There was a job called Landman—if you were a girl, they called you "Landma'am"—in which you traveled the courthouses of the rural west, trying to untangle mineral rights. Then you visited the people who owned them and tried to talk them into leasing. It sounded nosy and interesting, and until the oil business suffered one of its cyclical crashes, I got to do it in Kentucky and east Texas. After that, my father and I began trying to raise money, ostensibly to drill our own wells, but really just to maintain our tiny office on Race Street, where we spent most of our time going out for hot turkey sandwiches.

In truth, my father and his buzz words didn't get us anywhere. He was just as happy to stay home watching squirrels and listening to Wagner as to dress up in a suit and go out on a sales call.

So I was alone the day I hit up an oil baron's wife in one of those new suburban mansions. She chain-smoked silently through my entire spiel, making an occasional trip to the Mr. Coffee. When I finished, she changed subjects. She wanted to save me.

"Don't you see? One day soon the end of the world will come, and only those of us who truly believe in Jesus Christ will live on eternally."

"I'm an atheist," I explained. She didn't hold it against me. No doubt I didn't believe in God because no one had ever explained that Jesus Christ could wash me clean and see that I lived forever. "The Rapture could happen five minutes from now," she insisted. "There would be this tremendous sound and suddenly you'd be gone! Vanished! And I'd be sitting here."

I had nothing against fantasies. I was always daydreaming about joining the Allman Brothers Band. But this particular vision

I didn't get. Eternal life sounded as if it would lack dramatic tension.

"I'm a New York Jew," I said, describing myself that way for the first time.

I realized, though, that in some ways I had felt like a Jew since childhood. I was the Jew and Jenny was the WASP—that was how we divided up our family's cultural identities, and we considered it accurate, even though both our personas were based on appalling stereotypes. She was into horses, rode in a fox hunt, and was fascinated by old money and the taste that went with it. She was impressed by the stoic coolness found in some members of my mother's family. (Once she slammed my Aunt Laura's hand in the door of her car. "Open the door," Aunt Laura said, in an almost conversational tone, and Jenny did. There was no screaming.) Jenny taught herself these skills.

On the other hand, I thought WASPs were out to get me. Rich people made me nervous. I didn't really grasp that plenty of Jews were wealthy, too. If you argued with your family and burst into tears at the dinner table; if pleasant, polite conversation in which no one brought up things that were none of their beeswax made you nervous; if you never stopped thinking about food, you were a Jew. It wasn't necessary to point out that God had nothing to do with it.

Other oil people tried to save me after that. Their attitudes were solicitous, as opposed to pushy. At the very least, before a meal—a roast cooked at home, or a pork tender sandwich in the piney woods—they'd bow their heads and begin talking to Jesus as if he were a really generous guy they'd known out on the rig.

"Lord, we just ask you to think of us and anoint us with your love, and we just want to thank you for these nice folks we're visiting with here at this table, and the delicious food we've been blessed to eat."

For heaven's sake, I thought—Jesus didn't cook this meal! If I were in the kitchen right now, I'd be pissed.

WHEN I WASN'T wearing one of my two outfits from the Career section at Target, I tried to maintain my connection to the hippies and outcasts I used to know, to do something outside the mainstream. *Westword,* Denver's alternative paper, allowed me to attempt a music column. I wrote about an all-girl band called The Guys, and my story appeared within a few days. I don't know if anything has ever filled me with hope as much as that first byline. Hundreds of weekly columns followed. I got to interview Frank Zappa and Dickey Betts, an actual Allman Brother. I met Buddy Guy, the best living blues guitarist in the world, and I know it's unprofessional but I sat on his lap when he asked me to.

It wasn't a job—it didn't pay that well—and I never thought I was doing anything artistic, or that it even counted as real writing, but something about it made me start playing the piano again. It turned out I was good enough to sit in with Denver bands, which is how I met Ludwig, a very good bass player with a handlebar mustache. He looked like Clark Gable in a sharkskin suit. The band he played with was hot hot hot—a big band blues review with a horn section and paying gigs. You had to wear flashy vintage clothes to play with them, and pretty soon I owned a closet full of dresses with built-in hourglass figures. On the day I bought high heels in three different colors, I realized I was turning into a girl. Ludwig bought me red lipstick and drug store perfume. This phase didn't last very long, but while it did, it was intoxicating. So was the fact that he introduced me as his girlfriend.

Ludwig believed in domesticity. He'd spent the first six years of his life on a self-sufficient farm in Germany, and he knew how to sew, grow vegetables, and work wood. We moved into a house, not an apartment. We did couple things I'd never done before: eating huevos rancheros while reading the Sunday paper, shopping for rose bushes. I introduced him to my parents; we went to Chicago to visit his. His father had grown up in Ukraine, not far from Chotzie's birthplace, so I was curious. His father said he'd lived through Stalin's famine and World War II and hadn't been sorry to leave.

"The whole place was full of Jews," he explained. "They lie and cheat. You can't trust them. I try to stay away from them, even here."

"My family is Jewish," I said, "and so am I."

And, I thought, *you're an ignorant peasant son-of-a-bitch, and my Jewish family is* beyond *smarter than you.* He apologized, but I never trusted him or liked him ever again. He and Ludwig's mother tried, without much hope of success, to get us to think about Jesus. No chance.

At home, we worshiped Oblivia together. *Pot's okay, as long as it doesn't lead to the Hard Stuff.* Or that's what I heard when I was a teen, but by this time I thought the Hard Stuff was romantic, the sort of thing a true musician always does. (And they do. They still do.) There were mushrooms, but also cocaine and heroin, and we did stick the occasional needle into our arms—that was the real deal, the rush of all rushes. It was another little togetherness ritual, another thing we could handle because we were in love. But if the Hard Stuff comes on hard, it also wears off with sickening speed. There was always that moment when we were desperate for more, almost ready to betray each other.

It must have scared me on some level because after we got married, I gave up the Hard Stuff. We bought a house, grew tomatoes, and started a band of our own. As part of a semiresponsible couple, I worked as a full-time staff writer for *Westword* while Ludwig became a carpenter. I found that he filled me with a sense of security.

I also found that he liked to drink—any kind of sickening liqueur, the kind of thing we kept around to put in a dessert recipe or drizzle on top of a froufrou drink, would disappear in a day, even when I hid it under the sink. It put me off alcohol, but then I liked to wait until he left for the day and take up my old habit of binge eating. Apparently the four-hundred-pound woman couldn't be defeated, not even when Weight Watchers pumped another billion dollars into advertising and hired Fergie, the Duchess of York. Not when Oprah came on stage lugging sixty pounds of fat in a wheelbarrow. Not any time soon.

It's said that people take up religion to fill the holes inside them, those *God-shaped voids* you hear about. It's bullshit, condescending bullshit, even—God has no interest in patching up wounds, only in making the world huge and interesting. But by the time I married Ludwig, there were holes. I admit it.

As usual, the holes were balanced out by the appearances of Vroom. My writing job constantly surprised me with people who knew what they wanted. I got to live their lives for as long as the research continued, and at *Westword*, it could take weeks. Sometimes when I called someone for a quote, they'd ask me, "What's your slant?" But there never was one. It was impossible to know, or guess, until a source revealed itself.

There was Dave Emge, an inspector for Denver Health and Hospitals, who visited run-down dwellings where run-down people still lived, sometimes without electricity, sometimes because they were so old they didn't notice the roach-covered stove and the shingles hanging from the caved-in roof. I followed him around for a story called "Grime and Punishment." Every day, he put on pressed slacks and just a dab of cologne, and walked handsomely through genuine hovels where Dobermans growled at his heels and the smells were thick and horrible. He diagnosed rats, mice, and sadness. When he came upon a seventeen-year-old girl sitting in a cheap hotel room with two male crack addicts, he spirited her away to a shelter even when she said she didn't want to go.

"I just worry," he said to her. "You don't seem like a happy camper."

I had thought he was some kind of enforcer, but there was no punishment. I developed a crush on him, as anyone else would have done.

Stories weren't always that serious. Sometimes they were uplifting, though I never would have used a word like that in a story. There was Sal Herrera, a mariachi band leader, about sixty, who'd worked almost constantly since he was sixteen, driving back and forth across the country to any town with a Mexican community, stopping for meals and gas in places where people weren't used to seeing busloads of mariachis. He got stared at a lot, he said.

"But after a while, I started to like it," he told me. "I figured I was making people's day unusual. Who cares if they didn't know what to say to me? Who cares if I looked different? I like to open the door of some café and stand there for a minute. Then I say, 'Hello, all you lucky people! Here I am!'"

I wrote that down and put it on the bulletin board above my desk. It's still there.

It makes sense, in retrospect, that I never stuck with a religion that embraces the renouncing of worldly attachments. The more life I saw, the more limitless it seemed. I don't feel bad about this at all, or in any way underevolved. Jews seem to have concluded that life is all there is. That's what they drink to when they drink.

ONCE IN A great while, I passed as an investigative reporter. In the summer of 1989, Mike O'Keefe, in the next cubicle, was doing a story on the LaPorte Church of Christ, a white supremacist group thought to have been in cahoots with the Christian Identity zealots who ordered the murder of Alan Berg, an obnoxious, yet liberal talk show host. Mike wanted to get to know these Nazis, as he put it, but they wouldn't return his calls. They were, however, holding a summer retreat for families on the western slope of Colorado. Mike decided to infiltrate the camp but feared he'd stand out as a lone single man. Ideally, he wanted to be half of a married couple. I offered to play his wife because I was perfect for the role, five months pregnant and already fat enough for maternity clothes.

At the camp, Mike attended seminars such as "Biblical Banking: The Zionist Threat and What You Can Do About It" while I learned, step by step, how to plan a pleasant, nutritious dinner. You take a crayon and a piece of paper, and you make a dot the color of each food you plan to serve. Do all the colors go together? Is your meal unattractively beige? Were we being good "helpmeets" or did we plan to leave our family home *every single day* to pursue a "funsy little job"?

Polite-seeming white people had serious discussions about what to do with "niggers," whom they also called "mud people." The gist of the solution was to send them back to their own continent so that good Christians could concentrate on God's work. Managing the Jews was a bigger issue. They had wormed their way into every corner of the government. They controlled the World Bank. Sometimes they could even masquerade as racially pure because they were mostly white, and that's why you had to learn about racial characteristics. A practiced eye could spot Semitic features every time.

It was a terrible place to bring my unborn child. If they figured out who we were, I thought, we'd never get back to Denver. But I also felt proud—people like this had been trying to extinguish Jews forever, but it never worked because, as they admitted, we were diabolically smart.

At night, Pastor Pete Peters talked of Jesus, but only in passing, and I wasn't sure he knew any more about the son of God than I did. Jesus had accepted everyone, that much was clear, so what could he have in common with these idiots? If Jesus really was eternal, he suffered still, I imagined, from the things that were said and done in his name out there among the aspen trees.

When our story was published, the Christian Identity people put out a special issue of their white pride newsletter. Someone had drawn a cartoon of Mike and me. They got Mike exactly right, scraggly beard and all, even though they'd never met him. I came out as a skinny dame with a bad perm, long fingernails and a giant nose. Underneath the picture, the caption read, "Jewess Reporter."

THE MORE PREGNANT I got, the less I cared about night. What happened after sunset that I hadn't already seen? But Ludwig was still playing gigs, and one evening a few months before my baby was born, his band appeared nearby at a blues bar in North Denver, and I decided to go. Between sets, I went out for air with Joe, the owner of the club. Almost at the same time, we saw one of those little cocaine envelopes that used to be called a bindle. It was lying on the sidewalk, looking very pristine.

We were supposed to see free drugs as a gift from heaven, or something. On the other hand, they could easily be cut with Mexican baby laxative or elephant tranquilizer or good old baking soda. I was thinking about how uninterested I was—the bakery section at the all-night Safeway a few blocks away had won out as master of my illicit kicks—when Joe suddenly picked up the cocaine and emptied it elegantly out into the wind. As the little bits of powder blew away, we could see there had been quite a bit more than a gram. Hundreds of dollars worth of buzz, flying into the night.

A few weeks later, I woke up obsessed with scrubbing the kitchen floor, with Clifton Chenier's "Paper in My Shoe" playing over and over again on my record player. I retreated into myself, understanding that what was about to happen was a complete mystery. The floor was hygienically pristine when I finally went into labor.

Coco was an old soul at birth. She stared at me with huge blue eyes and calmed me down. *I know you. You're not as complicated as all that.* They took her away in a little rolling Lucite cradle. I immediately recognized the squeak of the right front wheel, and knew when she was coming back to me. I sat on the floor, holding her on my lap and staring at her. What divine thing this was I couldn't say, but Coco knew.

THE WORLD IS full of men who turn pale at the words "we need to talk." Fight or flight. They'd really rather not. You begin to feel cruel and unusual for suggesting it. All the same, I forced Ludwig to go with me to "see someone." I was afraid that if we didn't go, he'd leave me.

We learned to communicate using I-statements. (This was our favorite: *I* think *you're* an asshole. The therapist waited patiently for us to stop laughing.) We also learned what not to say, and that was easier, because marriage seemed to have eroded our ability to talk. We didn't feel abnormal about it, though. Lots of established couples had nothing to say to each other.

The marriage began its dissolve on the first day I met someone I could talk to. My editor put Eric at the desk next to me and asked me to try to get along with him, even though he struck me as a wiseass who threatened my supremacy as a riffer. I don't know what he thought of me, but we stayed away from each other for several months. But then, during a boring editorial meeting, we began to pass notes.

"Sure there's been all these advances in medical science," he wrote, "but what ever happened to The Humors? No one ever calls anyone 'choleric' anymore."

I replied: "What's wrong with you? You strike me as a sick individual. Or maybe Sikh."

Our endless chat took off and quickly lost control. We liked to go downtown, sit on a bench, imagine what the passers-by were thinking, and tell each other. We did accents. We did on-the-spot fashion makeovers, even though we were spending our lives in jeans and T-shirts. (The vintage dresses and high heels hadn't lasted long.)

"I think she should just pull it all together with a blazer," Eric was fond of saying.

We lobbied our office for corporate perks, even though—especially though—there was nothing corporate going on anywhere in editorial. Some companies have in-house cafeterias, we pointed out. Shouldn't they give us a man in a toque carving slabs of roast beef to order? Other companies provided steel-toed shoes. Were there any such things as steel-toed pumps?

We even discussed health and nutrition. While it's obviously prudent to limit animal fat consumption, there's no substitute for a mushroom cheeseburger so large you don't even want to know what it weighs. The bun should collapse into your fingers, meld into the meat. You should go through several napkins. What should the desire for this kind of food be called? We settled on "fatty passion."

We talked about writing—how to break out. We wrote a one-page porn masterpiece titled "Chitlins and Lace: An Appalachian Love Story." We wrote a one-*paragraph* porn masterpiece with a

Harley angle: "The Story of O Ring." We posted these efforts on the wall outside our cubicle, but no one much read them. It didn't matter. We couldn't imagine needing their opinions.

Of course we ended up having an affair, fueled by fatty and other passions, but what started it, what maintains it, what will probably wreck whichever one of us outlives the other, is the need for satisfying talk.

My psyche felt sandblasted, as if I were being reformatted to make disk space available. I heard music with a clarity I hadn't felt in years. The demigods I'd tangled with for years seemed to be fading into their corners. Ludwig found out, as did Eric's live-in girlfriend and then I was really in orbit, spinning around above my old life, rootless, and full of weird expectations. In the upheaval, God help me, I really felt pretty good.

Not trusting my instincts, I went to the local coffee house to see Lari, a psychic ex–moving man from Long Island. He wore Wiccan symbols around his neck and evangelized about Gurdjieff. The idea of him was comical, but the reality was comforting. You could unburden yourself in his incense-scented office, its walls so thin you could hear milk being steamed a few feet away.

He shuffled his Tarot cards absently and picked his teeth. Then he started dealing cards, throwing them down hard. Their edges were frayed, well-used.

"Huh," he said, as if receiving messages via lapel mike. "Whaddaya? Robin? You wanna go down into the *grave* with the father of your child? Is that it? Lemme tell ya, you don't know *one thing* about married happiness, even though you think you do. You're gonna find out though."

Infatuation was all very well, but I couldn't imagine married happiness with Eric, a never-married, childless guy who traveled the world, got together with his friends on weekend nights, climbed mountains, and biked to work from his bachelor pad. All those things a married parent couldn't seem to do. It made me defensive.

"You should own a house," I told Eric. "With our shitty salaries, it's the only investment you can afford. And a life without a child seems empty to me."

"And you have this desire to have everyone you ever met over for some kind of dinner party," he said. "It makes me very nervous."

We tried this line of talk, but kept returning to mutual kicks. He had a motorcycle, too. Maybe we could ride to Tierra del Fuego?

I would take only necessary objects. My cast-iron frying pan. My black-and-white composition notebook. Coco.

"I can't go without my daughter," I said.

"We'd need to get her a goose down vest. It gets cold in Tierra del Fuego."

We could talk about that, too.

Connection is divine. It can make you believe in God, even if you always thought he was nothing but a ridiculous distraction dreamed up by peasants who couldn't handle the nothingness. And that's what eventually happened.

My divorce was not yet final that New Year's Eve. I still lived in my married house and my daughter still saw her father every four days, although all that would change soon. I was driving through downtown Denver with Eric, thinking about the difference between Gene Kelly and Fred Astaire. Fred was dapper, precise and gentlemanly; Gene was muscle and khakis. I asked Eric which dancer he preferred.

"Oh, Gene Kelly," he said. I was so pleased. I was flooded by the rightness of his answer.

Seeing God is supposed to be accompanied by extreme weather. Instead, we got a gentle rain and the warm winter wind known as Chinook. I didn't hear anything cheesy like a disembodied voice, but I felt the presence of God in my veins. I don't know how else to explain it. I just did.

In the Torah, the patriarchs had just one thing to say whenever God called out to them: "*Hineini!* Here I am!"

That's what I thought. Here I am! Here I am! *We* are here, I thought, and nowhere else, in this moment. We're not just connected to each other but to everything else, which is huge. We're nothing but two little bits, connecting. Why does that feel so good when it sounds so depressing?

"Do you believe in God?" I asked him.

He had to think before he answered.

"Yeah," he finally said. "If not God, something."

Something like this moment, and in the next moment we could be hit by the proverbial bus, God being not a vengeful old man or the essence of serene nonstriving, but a current that runs through all things. You could step into it, almost by accident, and suddenly be caught up in it. And then how could you wonder if life has a purpose? It has a million.

What Does a Jew
Need to Know and Do?

Three years later, I looked up "synagogue" in the yellow pages and dialed Congregation Beth Evergreen, the only place listed in the small Colorado mountain town where we now lived. Eric and I were married and expecting a daughter. In fact, I was eight months pregnant.

I ended up on the phone with Rabbi Elliot Baskin. He asked me about myself.

"My husband and I are interested in God," I said. "We're looking for, uh, some information."

"Are you Jewish?" he asked.

"Maybe."

Rabbi Baskin suggested I call myself Jewish when I checked in to the hospital to have the baby. That way, Denver's Jewish community chaplain would be notified to visit me—and Denver's Jewish community chaplain just happened to be Rabbi Baskin. Evergreen was too small to have a full-time rabbi, and the chaplaincy was his second job.

He also pointed out that it was Sukkot, which I remembered from one of my grandfather's books. You built a hut outdoors on Sukkot—on Chotzie's Lower East Side, they did it on the fire escape—ate meals in it, and entertained guests. Some nice local people, the Wildenbergs, were hosting an open *sukkah*. Anyone could come party in their hut. I was considering taking down their address and attending my first organized Jewish activity, when Rabbi Baskin asked, "Do you sing?"

"Yes," I said. "Why?"

"We'll be singing all kinds of Jewish folk music! It's easy to learn!"

A Hebraic hootenanny? My feet grew cold. Folk music had always bugged me. In a debate of Pete Seeger vs. Muddy Waters, I'd back Muddy. There was more cultural anthropology than soul in those folk tunes, and besides, religious music was always so prone to an off-putting lack of hipness.

Speaking of which, as long as I was riffling through the phone book, why didn't I look up "church"? We could have become Friends or Unitarians—both fine religions—or we could just be *spiritual,* like so many other people I'd known. We could love nature and God in all things without losing our distrust of organized Judeo-Christianity. (If you're *spiritual,* it's okay to collect Zuni fetishes, but not to attend midnight Mass.) The truth is, we might have passed right over Judaism if it hadn't been for Eric's college roommate, Karen Holtz. He'd always called her Holtz.

Holtz had grown up Jewish in Boston. It was one of the first things anyone found out about her. Of course, this made Eric merciless: "Jew eat yet, Holtz? Jew seen my keys anywhere?" They played ultimate Frisbee and rugby together, and by junior year they were sharing a house off campus. Because Holtz talked about herself a lot, her needs were always clear. Here's what she wanted as an adult: to marry a nice Jewish boy with *red* hair and *wide* shoulders, to have *two* kids, to be a marine biologist, and to go to a Dead show every year until she died. She was the kind of friend who kept in touch, and Eric was always up on the progress of these various goals. He had been hiking and climbing mountains with her ever since they left college.

By the time I met her, Holtz, then in her early thirties, was working in Portland, Oregon, and holding yearly Passover seders for crowds of people, Jewish and otherwise. She hadn't made much progress on the red-headed Jewish family, but was happy with her friends and sporting obsessions. At five foot tall and 100 pounds, she was a small but tough competitor on the state cycling circuit. When she came to Colorado for our wedding, she spent two hours in the garage with six-year-old Coco, performing a custom bike fit on a Wal-Mart cruiser. She liked kids.

Four months later, during a Sunday morning training ride, she was hit by a drunk driver and suffered massive brain injuries. Eric went immediately to Oregon to be with the Holtzes as they disconnected their daughter from life support; then he reversed directions and went to Cape Cod for the funeral because Jewish bodies must go quickly into the ground. She was buried in a Jewish cemetery under the name *Keren* Holtz—she'd recently switched to the Israeli spelling of her first name. Eric and his friend Steve Albert were the only people Holtz's age who knew about the tragedy in time to attend. It was a hot, blue day, perfect for Cape Cod sailing, another thing Holtz had loved to do. The rabbi in charge handed Eric and Steve shovels and asked them to pile dirt on top of Holtz's coffin, even though the custom is usually to let each person throw one shovelful. Instead, the rabbi gave Steve and Eric the entire job.

It was good to move, Eric said, to sweat a little, to be useful. When you've had enough emotional labor, a little physical work is a relief.

"We have good reasons for most of our traditions," the rabbi explained.

"Maybe we should be Jews," Eric said, when he got home. You have to like reasonable traditions.

(We've since heard of some ridiculous ones. What good reason is there to swing the carcass of a dead chicken around and around your head on Yom Kippur? Can sins really pass magically into a capon? Needless to say, this was a Jewish tradition we rejected.)

At Holtz's funeral, no one had suggested that she was now doing hundred-mile rides in heaven or that she'd gone to a better place. She was just turning into human compost in a quiet, grassy graveyard in Falmouth. Her life had been short, but purposeful and passionate. One summer she had had a job walking upstream in hip waders counting salmon because they were dwindling, and her impossible goal—her actual paid job—was to bring them back.

Maybe we should be Jews. Hence, the yellow pages.

Once we were looking, Judaism made cameo appearances in newspaper articles and books, even in the HBO series *Six Feet Under,* where a glamorous female rabbi said: "One day of this life is worth a thousand in eternity." One day of this life has intriguing possibilities. You can look upon food, family, mindless riffing, and even sex as something God wants you to enjoy. Sublimating desire doesn't make you a better Jew. It's an interesting matter of theology: Christians see sex as the number one sin that took place directly after Adam and Eve were expelled from Eden; Jews think it happened before, when the young couple lived in paradise, of which sex should certainly be a component. Jewish sex has nothing to do with sin unless you do it with the wrong person. (Or, for the Orthodox, at the wrong time of month.) Ancient Jewish texts guarantee the right not just to sexual frequency, but satisfaction, especially for women. The Mishnah spells out how often we may expect to get lucky according to what our husbands do for a living. If he's a camel driver—the Biblical world's equivalent of a long-haul trucker—every thirty days; if a Torah scholar, once a week; every day if a man of leisure. And if you don't use this gift, you could actually hurt God's feelings—in the same way that he's insulted if you fail to notice one of his mountain ranges.

The more traditional Jews exit the world in plain white garments, in cheap pine caskets, as quickly as possible. No embalming, no cremation, no taking wealth with you into the beyond. I recognized this as sane. I was always more drawn to black earth than ashes. I always thought that when you die, it's over. This is an acceptable thing for a Jew to think.

The Evergreen synagogue met at a Methodist church. In 1998, Evergreen wasn't big enough for a real temple, but a small group of local Jews had been together for nearly thirty years, first in living rooms, then in community buildings, and now at a church.

They were slowly increasing. But we were spooked by the specter of folk music and so put off joining them. One month later, we had a daughter, and rather than give her a name that started with the same letter as that of a favorite dead relative, as many Jews do, we named her Augusta McCrae, after the cowboy hero of *Lonesome Dove*. We called her Gus.

Nearly a year later, we finally went to our first Jewish service. The October rain was appropriately solemn—these were the High Holy Days, whatever that meant. Rosh Hashanah had begun the previous night at sundown. All I knew was that this was a big day for a Jew, possibly full of awe.

No one displayed it. People filed into the sanctuary (where the cross had been propped against a far wall), and ushers were setting up chairs to hold the overflow. It was 9:30 A.M., time for the service to start, but no one paid attention. They milled around, chatting, their children running around as if this were a massive play date.

The congregation was as big as it would get on any day of the year. A preponderance of Jews go to synagogue just three times a year, but I didn't know that yet, either. I just thought, wow— Evergreen has three hundred Jews? Amazing.

We braced for the religious come-on, the basket passing, the "welcome, neighbor!" But it never came. I began to think Christians were friendlier than these people. They'd lend you their Bible so you could read along. Jews were downright standoffish if you hadn't met them and didn't know where to go or what to say when.

A guitar player was tuning up by the altar; a short man with dark, curly hair was testing a lapel mike, à la Jay Leno. This was

Rabbi Elliott Baskin. I'd never seen either of these guys before, but as I looked around, I spotted a few familiar people. The assistant tennis pro from the health club. Another mom from day care. Two guys from the volunteer fire department Eric had recently joined. Their being Jewish was a subject that had absolutely never come up.

The room began to quiet down. I was fascinated by the prosperous-looking men in yarmulkes—doctors? real estate agents?—unzipping ornate velvet bags, removing silk scarves with fringes, *kissing* the fringes, and putting the shawls over their shoulders, as if creating a small tent in which to pray. It was as much an exotic costume as the robe of a Russian Orthodox priest. A few women put on prayer shawls, too—these tended more toward the Boulder tie-dye than the ancient Semitic.

Around us, people started to read their prayer books in earnest, plowing through big chunks of text. I opened mine and saw it was about equal parts Hebrew and English, only one of which I could understand. The first song could have been in Hebrew, but maybe it was Yiddish. Who knew? Once Rabbi Baskin shushed the crowd—and not for the last time—we followed along in the prayer books, page after page, repeating the Hebrew prayers with the help of transliterations. *Baruch atah Adonai eloheinu, melech ha-olam?* Clues were packed below the line in the form of commentary, so that even as we ingested prayers and Torah, we could read alternate interpretations, poetry, the thousand-year-old teachings of a long-gone rabbi, even Judy Chicago and a Muslim poet. The rabbi was there not as a spiritual leader so much as the director of a large, noisy study hall.

I got that the High Holy Days had to do with repentance of sins, but here a "sin" was known as a *chayt,* and that word had started out as an archery term. All it meant was "missing the mark." Yom Kippur seemed to be for confronting the times you'd done that in the previous year. It had nothing to do with your essential beastliness, or even, necessarily, a breaking of commandments. A *chayt* was helping my father engage in the activity he called "stirring the pot," carrying interesting gossip between warring family members. (There was even a Yiddish word for a person who does this: *kochlefl,* or literally, "big spoon.") A *chayt* was sharing adult angst with Coco, when it was none of her business and would only burden her the way my father had burdened me. I was asked to think about this, and to make amends as soon as possible.

Jews all over the world were doing approximately the same thing, but not always in the open. Maybe that's why the rabbi led us in a prayer for the Jews of Russia. Obviously, practically everyone else in the room had Eastern European roots like mine—Lower East Side relatives who'd come from Russia, grown up poor, but died as successful dentists and musicians and writers, with children who never saw the old country. What happened to the ones who stayed behind? If they lived through Stalin and didn't end up in a mass grave in a Lithuanian forest, how were they holding up in a place where Jews have always been blamed for trouble? Maybe they gave up their Jewish identity and faded into the crowd.

The woman next to me handed me a Kleenex. I was in the middle of an embarrassing cry—runny nose, red eyes, wet prayer book. I thought: *Am I responsible for my fellow man? Yes. Enlightened self interest, blah blah blah. Fuck all that. I'm a Jew, and my family is bigger than I would have thought. Life is going to get complicated now, but that's okay. If I look out for them, they'll look out for me.*

The service lasted four hours. My butt was numb by the time it was over, but oddly enough my brain was wide awake, digesting the whole Jewish New Year concept. There was a lot to do—celebrate all of creation, feel brand new about everything old, start over, acquire a few cosmic points. You have to admit you're human; that you will probably screw up again next year, but that your desire to make things right is believable. For the next ten days—until Yom Kippur, the day of atonement—that would be our work, but no two Jews agreed on how to do it properly. In person and in the pages of the prayer book, they argued and split hairs and said, "Yes, but here's another way of looking at it." I was sitting among my own people for a change, even if they didn't notice I was there.

PICKING A RELIGION is supposed to involve zeal and fervor, both of which sounded great. What's not to like about life-changing transformation? But that's not how it happened. Rather than becoming a born-again Jew, I wandered over in the direction of Judaism and stayed there until I got used to it. Eric was there too, which didn't hurt. But, frankly, it was a crapshoot. *Oh, this,* I thought, without the slightest hint of a thunderclap or revelation. *I can live with this. I belong here.*

There was no need to broadcast it, either. My family would think I had completely lost my mind, and my friends would worry. Religion was turning out to be a touchy hobby, more isolating than my previous enthusiasms. When I took up playing the banjo, ballroom dancing, or snowboarding, I engaged with all kinds of people, had conversations about gear, made dates. But I couldn't talk about my particular God, not only because people were suspicious, but because I didn't know anything.

December 1999 was a travesty. I bought a menorah and blue-and-white candles, made in Israel, at Bed Bath & Beyond, but I hated not to bring out my secular tree ornaments, so I compromised and bought a large willow branch to hang them on, and our schizophrenic display stayed up from Chanukah through December 25—several weeks. After that, I put the box of ornaments in the basement and we broke it off with Christmas. I bought a book called *Jewish Family and Life* and tried to memorize the "Rules and Regs" section. I left the book sitting out in the living room. One day my sister Jenny spied it.

"What is *this*?" she said. A look shot between her and her son Nick. "What does this mean? You guys are converting! You're going to *convert!* I can't believe this!"

This was part of a shocking trend. Friends she thought reasonable and pragmatic turned up wearing crucifixes. They had their babies baptized and went to Bible study. She felt incredulous, but also a little left out. Was everyone a moron, or were they seeing things she couldn't see, and if so, why couldn't she? Science had no explanation for any of it, and if I didn't know that, it wasn't because I hadn't been taught.

"What does she mean, *convert*?" my father asked. (The shocking news, thanks to faithful pot stirring, had already spread around the family.) "You're already a Jew, aren't you? I'm a Jew, you're at least half a Jew."

Actually, so was Eric. Although his father's family had belonged to a Methodist church in Bedford Hills, New York, for generations, his mother, Betsy, was a Jew who had grown up in New York City among old-country relatives who worked in the garment business as tailors, milliners, and dress shop owners, and literally got things for her wholesale. The reason this wasn't immediately apparent, that Eric wasn't much aware of his mother's Jewishness, was that Betsy's father, Louis Hacker, had been a sort of academic Chotzie. He had grown up with his own set of *goyish* passions and was driven to climb as high as he could at prestigious colleges and universities. It wasn't all that different from the music world—if you wanted to get there, you left Judaism behind. Louis married a Jewish woman, Lily Lewis, but she died of cancer when Betsy was fourteen, by which time Betsy had entered a boarding school in England. Her father and brother joined her in England—Louis taught at Oxford—and, back at boarding school, Betsy received a rudimentary education in Anglican Christianity. Not long after that, the family returned to New York City, and Betsy left religion behind until she was married to Roy Dexheimer by a nondenominational minister, in a nondenominational chapel at Columbia University, where her father had recently founded the School of General Studies.

Nevertheless, when she had three children, she took them to church. "It was just what mothers did back then," she remembers. "We wore hats and little gloves, too, if that gives you an idea." Betsy was looking for a minister concerned with social justice—

not necessarily an easy task in Batavia, the western New York town where the Dexheimer family now lived. Eric remembers a rotation of everything from black, full gospel services to Catholic masses. He ended up being confirmed at a small Presbyterian church Betsy had come to like. His memories of the ceremony mostly involve a beautiful teenage babysitter his parents had hired to stand in for them because they were in the Soviet Union at the time.

"I was the coolest kid there, walking down the aisle with this older blond woman," he remembers. "The other kids just had parents."

After confirmation, Eric stopped going to church, which was fine with Betsy. At that point, she left it up to him. Most of his friends were Catholic. Batavia's few Jews worshiped at a small synagogue manned by a visiting rabbi—Eric went to one bar mitzvah and was impressed by the envelopes of money old men kept slipping into the boy's pocket.

I'd never been to a bar mitzvah, myself. Or a bat. Until my early forties, I'd never even been inside a synagogue. Strangely, though, a few Passover seders had been held at my Jewish grandmother's house, because my 100 percent Jewish-by-blood cousin, Lisa, had heard about the holiday and thought it sounded interesting. Her father, who had been raised Orthodox, led us through the Maxwell House *haggadah,* reading the prayers in the fluent Hebrew he'd learned as an Orthodox boy. He taught us to sing *Had Gadya* and hunt for the *afikomen.* It was a big, noisy feast, like Thanksgiving, and we all liked it enough to keep it going for several years. But was it religious? No. Even though Lisa sort of wanted it to be.

So, my father wanted to know, if you grew up not believing in God, why the hell would you start? Why would you foist that bullshit on your children? Religious people in general were weird, but there was nothing weirder than a religious Jew.

I had to think if I'd ever met one. I'd *seen* one: the occasional Chasid in a hot wool suit in an airport. I had been surrounded by religious people at Beth Evergreen. Holtz, of course, had been a Jew, but didn't go to synagogue much as an adult.

Who else?

Sarah Steinberg.

Sarah had a cable access TV talk show in the mid-1980s, when I had just started working at *Westword*. It was called *Something Special with Sarah Steinberg*. I went to interview her and ended up a guest on the show. She was only eighteen, but matronly before her time, her hair sprayed stiff, her makeup mask-like. She'd grown up in the last remaining pocket of West Denver's Jewish neighborhood, worked in her parents' kosher deli, and played piano by ear at the age of three. Somehow she'd been raised in a vacuum. Her modern cultural references extended to the Bee Gees and Amy Grant, both of whom she admired tremendously.

Something Special was an old-fashioned variety hour. Sarah played old Yiddish songs on the piano and hosted such guests as Darryl Ha, a Soviet immigrant whose talent was blowing soap bubbles. Another young Chasid, looking aged and pasty, played "Bei Mir Bist Du Schön" on an electronic keyboard while Sarah sang harmony. Occasionally she'd get a visitor from the secular world—Justin Mitchell, music critic for the *Rocky Mountain News*.

Or me. A mysterious woman known as Helen Fay, Queen of the Yiddish Theater—mysterious because there *was* no Yiddish Theater—appeared more often than anyone else. After these guests performed, they joined Sarah on a Merv Griffith–like living room set, and she asked them questions such as, "Tell me, Justin, when do you think disco will come back?"

"Never, I hope," Justin said.

Sarah ignored him. She couldn't conceive of a world that had forgotten about the Bee Gees. Of course they would come back. (Of course, she was right.)

I wrote a story about Sarah—a you're-in-the-audience-at-the-talk-show story. But that wasn't the end, because she called me every time her career got an infinitesimal boost. It happened all the time, so there was plenty to talk about. She loved publicity and had some idea how to manipulate it. She knew, for instance, that I found her fascinating but bizarre, and would probably invite my readers to gawk at her along with me. Wisely, she didn't trust me, and kept her eye on the notes I was taking, correcting every mistake. And I ended up writing two more stories about her. They began to feel like chronicles—full of family and big musical themes, as well as a backstage look at a culture that seemed to be dying. Who was an Orthodox Jew in this day and age?

The Steinbergs were a showbiz family. Daily life was necessary but annoying, as if they were marking time between production numbers. The future rested on Sarah. The oldest son, Dov, had already moved to Chicago for an arranged marriage, and Moish, the middle son, was a dependable worker, but Sarah had the talent.

Mrs. Steinberg, who had had her kids rather late in life, chronicled every moment of Sarah's ascent—the talent contests, the gigs at the Jewish senior centers. It was like an Orthodox production of *Gypsy* in that Mrs. Steinberg didn't seem to want to give up her own theatrical ambitions. She broke into song around the deli and videotaped *Rope,* an elaborate handheld horror movie, starring herself, with her three kids in cameo roles.

Her small moment of fame had come forty years earlier. As a teenager in Taunton, Massachusetts, she had entered and won a woodchopping contest. The wisecracking newspaper interviews she did—"no palookas for husbands, that's my motto!"—got some play on the East Coast. Sarah had the clips to prove it, and when the fortieth anniversary of the woodchopping victory came around, she alerted both Johnny Carson and David Letterman, both of whom booked Mrs. Steinberg immediately. Sarah sat in the green room while her mother went out on the set to act eccentric and unintentionally hilarious. A hit! My next Sarah story came shortly after she returned from New York.

It had been a wonderful, all expense paid trip—almost dreamlike in its intensity. She'd felt perfectly comfortable around Carson and Letterman, as she called them. The minute she'd mentioned her love of the Bee Gees, someone gave her tickets to see them that night at Madison Square Garden. The new songs she wrote about the experience dwarfed her previous repertoire. "Taunton," a torchy single, was a novelty hit on that town's radio station for a while, and Sarah was quite sure this would lead to fame, but even then she promised not to sell out. She would remain an observant girl, the Jewish Amy

Grant. She was working behind the deli counter when she made this promise.

I had come by on a Friday afternoon. Not knowing anything about the coming Sabbath, I wondered why the store was so crowded with frantic young housewives towing their children through narrow aisles, dressed in long skirts and Barbra Streisand–style wigs. They looked disapprovingly at my tank top. I was the only woman in the place with naked arms.

After I watched Sarah's mother for a while, I became suspicious.

"Hey," I whispered to Sarah, "is she Helen Fay, Queen of the Yiddish Theater?"

Sarah couldn't deny it.

"What about your father? Has he ever been on the show?"

"No, he travels a lot."

"What does he do?"

"He's a *sofer.*"

In other words, he had the rare, old-country skill of inscribing lambskin Torah scrolls by hand. One job could take nearly a year. Sarah showed me a picture—her father was old, with a long white beard, a rumpled black suit, and Ellis Island eyes. He'd been born in Poland and survived the camps. So how had he met and married the Taunton Woodchopping Champion?

I figured I had plenty of time to find out the answer. I saw no reason not to chronicle Sarah's life until we were both too old to perform our respective *shticks*. But the last Steinberg story I wrote concerned her family's sudden decision to move to New York City for the sake of Sarah's career. Within weeks, the deli was sold and the apartment in the projects, where they'd lived since 1969, was empty. Sarah said she was no longer impressed by Denver. She already had big contacts in New York City, and for all I know she could be a star of the Jewish music world by now. But Googling her, I find only a small mention of the Sarah Steinberg Happy Music Center, somewhere in the 718 area code.

Sarah was the only observant girl I ever met, unless there were others who didn't choose to mention it. A single conversation about God would have crossed the line with me. But now I wonder how I could have treated the central fact of her life as such an oddity.

THE WRITER JOANNE Greenberg is a founding member of Congregation Beth Evergreen, but I didn't meet her there. I came to her as a newspaper reporter, shortly after my first official High Holy Days. Beth Evergreen had decided to raise money for its own synagogue building, which would make it the first in our county. It sounded like one of those boilerplate, topic-sentence local news stories, and I happened to need one for my *Westword* column. Rabbi Baskin and CBE president Dave Froman gave me the details, but said I wouldn't understand the temple until I called Joanne. The synagogue was a hard place to pigeonhole, particularly for Jews who'd grown up Orthodox or in a large Reform congregation. Rabbi Baskin liked to call it "Reconservadox." It was a good word for Joanne, too, who was a writer and also one of the original mountain Jews. Being a sucker for a famous writer— imagine having written *I Never Promised You a Rose Garden*—I couldn't wait to see how she lived. Maybe I could learn something about the craft—what she ate, what computer she used, how all those years of sitting alone in a room putting sentences together hadn't driven her loopy.

Her house was only six miles away, a small 1960s-style *Sunset* magazine cabin on top of a mountain. My immediate impression was of books and tools, of homesteading supplies. I wasn't far off—it turned out Joanne made her own quilts, fermented her own wine, dipped her own candles, canned enough tomato sauce to last entire winters, and sewed her husband, Albert's, clothes, even his boxers.

We greeted each other in matching outfits, old pants with faded knees and flannel shirts. She looked more like my mother than my mother ever did. We ate pound cake and drank coffee, and I felt instantly at ease because Joanne didn't care that I knew nothing about Judaism and had to start from the beginning. In fact, she'd read some of my stories in *Westword* and wanted to know about me as much as I wanted to know about her. So we traded details for a while. She told me she wrote on a yellow legal pad, with a Mongol no. 4 pencil, for one-and-a-half hours every day.

"I get up, I go to the john, and I write," she said. "Any more than that and you could rupture something."

Someday, when no editors were breathing down my neck, I would try it myself. I could see myself living Joanne-style, maintaining my woodlots with a chainsaw, canning, sewing, gardening, and reading like a fiend. We had both become seriously rural, even though we'd both grown up in Manhattan—if you can imagine, less than one block apart.

"Except you grew up nothing, and I grew up Jewish," she said, "and that's different. How Jewish were we, though? Well, we lit candles on Friday night and said the blessings. We made a rapid appearance in the synagogue on the High Holy Days. But Judaism was old-country stuff, orthodox—all kinds of poverty and despair seemed to cling to it."

Joanne was interested in other things. She learned to tell stories in the Gullah dialect and play the dulcimer, and in 1956, at age twenty-two, she married Albert Greenberg and moved fearlessly to the Colorado foothills. She'd been to Colorado before, as a camp counselor, and felt she belonged there. On Lookout Mountain, she was first a mother of two young boys, trapped without a car through long mountain winters, then an elementary school teacher and volunteer firefighter, and finally, a working writer. Her most famous book, *I Never Promised You a Rose Garden,* was published in 1964. Her first book, *The King's Persons,* had been less of a blockbuster. It told the story of the York Massacre of Jews in the Middle Ages. And yet, for many years, there was nothing personally Jewish in her life.

No relatives called, no racial memory rekindled itself. She became religious almost by spontaneous combustion and has trouble pinning down how and when it happened. "Some people are religious, which is not to say better," she told me. "Religion is just a flavor—either you taste it or you don't. My husband, Albert, doesn't; I do. Simple."

Using library books, she taught herself Hebrew. After a few years, she was able to conduct the High Holy Days services by herself, in a rock quarry. She began a lifelong practice of keeping her own particular Greenberg Shabbat—no driving, cooking, carrying money, or talking on the phone, and certainly no writing. But if Albert should offer her a ride in his Packard, she sometimes accepts. It was all right, she remembered, being a one-woman congregation, but she wanted both her sons to have bar mitzvahs, and wasn't sure how to get that done.

Before long, she got a call from a rabbi in Kansas City.

"He said he'd enjoyed *The King's Persons* and asked if he could do anything for me," Joanne remembered, "and I told him all my troubles. Two days later, a whole package of books arrived—how to do the bar mitzvah, how to teach my children. Then he said, 'Your sons don't have enough Jewish contact. Send them to me for part of every summer.' And I did. This man was one of the diamond souls sprinkled throughout the world." Her sons went back East for their bar mitzvahs and "sang like birds."

The next phone call came from Bernie Goldman, a local guy working his way through the phone book. "I'm on a Jew hunt," he explained. Bernie got Joanne and a handful of other local Jews to meet once in a while to take turns running services and arrange their own bar mitzvahs and weddings. No one wanted anything to do with the ostentatious religions of their childhoods—the fur coats and the overload of fancy food set against a backdrop of pompously meaningless services held in synagogues that could have been mistaken for Protestant churches.

"Most of us were running hell-bent from exactly that. It was a good place for me. Although once I did get a call from someone inviting me to a Yom Kippur party," Joanne said, "and that was a little much. You don't exactly celebrate on a day like that."

There wasn't much frippery. When Beth Evergreen acquired its Torah—an eastern European scroll inscribed in the early 1900s—Albert built an ark for it using *Popular Mechanics* gun cabinet plans. The day I met Joanne, the Torah was living at her house, wrapped in a quilt she'd made from 1950s hospital gowns. She carried it down from a shelf and spread it out on the bed.

"She's a Holocaust survivor," Joanne said. "It's proper to call a Torah 'she.'"

She was one of the most mysterious artifacts in our town. Her pages were to be touched and read only with a tiny silver hand mounted on a stick—a *yod*. Hebrew words are all consonants, and if that doesn't make it difficult enough, there is no punctuation. Joanne said she'd learned to read from this Torah because if you read the original, you get to understand the jokes and puns.

"Jokes and puns?" I asked.

"Yes. You like languages?"

I did. In my haphazard schooling, I'd studied French, Spanish, German, and Russian, and had recently flirted with Portuguese.

"Have I got a language for you!" She rummaged through a closet and found me some elementary-school Hebrew workbooks. It turned out she'd taught Hebrew school for years—guiding our town's preteens through their bar and bat mitzvahs. By now the congregation had grown so big there was barely room for students in Joanne's living room, but that's where she still taught. Even if the proposed synagogue should be built, she said, she'd continue to teach at home.

The informal spirit of the Bernie Goldman days was fading. Dues, once six dollars per year, had increased to nearly a thousand.

There was a part-time rabbi and talk of affiliating with one of the organized branches of Judaism. But then, the whole town's population had quadrupled since 1956, and some of these new people had money. If they could pay for it, they'd get their building.

Which is what I had gone there to talk about, but it was just a structure and what more could be said about it?

"Do you go to all the events at the synagogue?" I asked her.

"No, and neither will you." I hadn't explained my transformation from rational person to believer. She just seemed to know. I tasted that flavor she talked about.

"Do you believe in unconditional love?" I asked Joanne.

"Nope," she said. "Only God can do that."

IN THE SPRING, without ever changing his position on religion being horseshit, my father called up to plan Passover. He had the menu all figured out—roasted capons, gefilte fish, herring, and those matzos and bitter herbs and all that, if you feel you must. He instructed us to produce a couple of *haggadahs*. Eric and I wrote one—as full of E. B. White and Adam Gopnik as Maimonides and Hillel. When Dad arrived, the table was formally set for five, including one high chair, but we hadn't yet learned to invite a stranger into our midst, which was a Jewish tradition on any holiday, especially the Sabbath. It made sense when you considered that even over thousands of years, Jews couldn't seem to stop being strangers themselves, and were often grateful for a free, friendly meal. Dad wore a baseball cap turned backward as a yarmulke, and sat at the head of the table.

"I'm the patriarch," he said. "Let's get this show on the road."
And we read through the Exodus story—Eric, my father, Coco,
Gus in her high chair, and me. Because the Jews had been re-
deemed from slavery, they celebrated with abandon when they finally crossed over the Sea of Reeds into freedom, although if
they'd known what servitudes would come next they might have
held back a little. A lot of Egyptians had drowned during the dramatic escape, and no Jew is supposed to entirely rejoice when another human suffers. But so what. It was finally spring, the perfect
time to celebrate liberty. My bedding plants—yellow and white
pansies with purple eyes—sat on the table in plastic six-packs.
Pesach, so tied to feasting, was better than Easter. No contest.
How could you not respect your ancestors for having survived
and ultimately flourished so many thousands of years ago? And
how Jewishly complicated God was turning out to be, constantly
messing with Pharaoh—hardening his heart, thawing it out, hardening it again, turning him into the first dysfunctional daddy of
history. How was this right? Who could make sense of it? How
thrilling that so many Jews would be debating this at this exhilarating time of year.

My father added his own learned commentary: grudgingly, he
approved of the *haggadah* because it wasn't preachy and contained
so few references to God.

"The only good part of being a Jew is the humor and the
food," he said. "I'm not interested in the rest."

I told him to think of it as an annoying hobby, as square as
square dancing. A thing humorless white people would do at

VFW halls. It didn't feel like that to me, but I thought the image might work for him.

WE POPPED BY the synagogue once in a great while. I had been shocked to learn that people who spent a lot of time there wrote checks to join. It explained the absence of a collection plate, but was steep, all the same. Nonpaying visitors, we skulked into temple and seldom got into conversations other than the brief hellos that came during the hokey moment when Rabbi Baskin said: "Now, I'd like you to take your hand, extend it in front of you, and shake hands with the first person you see."

Only the music assured me I was in the right place—not the folksy Jewish summer camp songs that reminded me of the schlocky modern hymns at Christian services, which I was barely willing to put up with, but the thready, minor-key chants that were sad and ancient-sounding and got me right in the *kishkes,* as my father would say. Their meaning was clear: *Because life can be hard, we must sing loud, play that guitar, get lost in music until our hearts are bare and our souls are clean and God has heard us.*

I had been drawn to blue notes forever, and when I started playing them, they came easily. Once I sat in with a Chicago guy and was surprised when he pegged me instantly as a Jew. "We both just wandered off from the twelve lost tribes," he said, "and *you* got the blues, baby."

At the time, I liked that a lot. Now I loved it.

Most of the people at services knew the songs. It made me happy to think that Gus, having been born Jewish, would soon know them herself, and that Coco could catch up a lot faster than I could. It was time to send her to Hebrew school, to write the first of many checks. Coco was ten—four years behind the other kids in Hebrew language, Torah stories, holidays, all of it. If she hadn't seen *Prince of Egypt* in day care, she would have been completely lost, but she didn't mind, and that didn't surprise me.

Coco's relationship with God had disconcerted me almost from the day she was born. Luckily, she waited until she was three to start bugging me about cosmic things.

"What *are* we?" she asked me then. "Susan's a Christian. They have coloring books at her church. What are we?"

Ludwig and I tried to squash this line of questioning—our total distrust of faith was one thing we had in common. Growing up in Germany, he'd had the crap scared out of him by nuns—devils, damnation, and frying in hell if you weren't a good boy. And he wasn't a good boy. One year he got a switch and a lump of coal in his Christmas stocking.

Eventually Coco heard these cautionary stories. They didn't make a dent.

"Why don't we believe in God?" she asked, at four, five, and six.

"Because there's no proof," I said. "People make up God to explain things they don't understand, but we mostly understand it all now."

"Why?"

"Because we know a lot. A lot of scientists know a lot."

"Why?"

"Because they study hard."

"Why?" Okay, I thought, these are nothing but aggravating preschool questions. *Why* is lettuce green? *Why* do I have to go to bed? *Why* don't you like Barbie? She'd grow out of it. Right?

I managed to get my mother worked up about this, too. She bought Coco a book about God that was so vague and nonsectarian as to make no sense at all. *There may be God and there may not, but people believe what they believe and we all live together on the planet, blah blah blah.* Coco let me read her the book. Once. It didn't satisfy her at all.

"But why is there God?" she asked.

"There *isn't!*"

"You don't know that." And then, "What *are* we?"

"We're nothing," I said.

"Huh."

Coco entered Hebrew school as if it were a nice, hot bath. The teachers loved her—they went out of their way to tell me so. Teachers always love Coco, I told myself, but she doesn't love school. No way did she have the motivation to catch up to her class in Hebrew on her own. I brought her to Hebrew school at the Methodist church every Wednesday afternoon anyway, as an act of faith. While she learned about Chanukah and the Ten Commandments, sang songs about apples and honey, and participated in games of Jewpardy, I talked to other parents in the parking lot, usually fathers. They were a cynical bunch—all of them had hated Hebrew school. "Between you and me," they'd say, "it's all kind of silly. All that memorizing in a dead language, and for what—so you can have a big party when you turn thirteen? So you can collect the checks?"

"And grow up and get married and send your own kids to Hebrew school?" I asked.

"Well, yes," one dad said. "At this age, there's an empty space
in their spirituality, and I want to make sure it gets filled with the
right information."

"So you're doing this to inoculate your son against being a
Hare Krishna?"

The dad gave me a tolerant look. I later found out he was a rational emotive therapist.

A few months into Coco's first year, a consecration ceremony
was held as part of a Friday night service, to welcome the kinder-
gartners—and one fourth-grader—into the community of learn-
ers. Coco was given a plastic Torah scroll. She kept it in a special
place next to her knock-off American Girl dolls. When I asked her
what she was learning, she said, "Oh, nothing."

A few months later, we drove past a homeless man holding a
cardboard sign. "Family of five. Hungry! Please help."

"Why didn't you give him money?" Coco asked. Ah, it was
time for *that* big life lesson: He might not really be hungry, he
might not have a family, he might spend the money on drugs,
there were shelters and meals and jobs available for him.

She thought it over, and then said: "It says in the Talmud that
while you're arguing about whether a guy is hungry or not he can
starve to death."

There was the immediacy of Judaism again, one of the main
things I loved about the religion. And it went, as the saying goes,
from Coco's lips, through me, to God's ear.

The next time we drove down to Denver, we brought a paper bag containing five peanut butter sandwiches and five Cokes. Coco had convinced me that packing milk instead of pop would be holier-than-thou.

"What?" my father said. "You're getting *her* all mixed up with religion?"

"Well, Judaism is more about the home than the synagogue. Coco's part of my home."

"Jesus."

That year we were sixteen at the Pesach dinner. Almost half of the guests had been born Jewish, but only Eric and I were practicing—officially out of the closet, if anyone cared to notice. My father had lured his friends with the promise of a funny, no-proselytizing ritual, and it was. We'd established a family tradition of ending the seder with a group recitation of that so-appropriate-motto for any Jewish holiday: *They tried to kill us, we won, let's eat!* As we raised our wine glasses, Coco, who was hidden on the stairwell, struck up "Hava Nagila" on her violin.

She knew a lot and was learning more. Eric and I were shamed. We signed up for a two-year course: the Florence Melton Adult Mini-School, where we read and discussed Maimonides and Yitz Greenberg, as well as *goyish* writings—Aristophanes and the Passion Plays—that had ventured opinions about the Jews. The very first class consisted of an argument: Did God put Adam and Eve in the Garden of Eden so that they could rule over all the creatures of the earth? Or so that they could care for the world and everything in it? Dominion or custodianship? There was no right answer. Voices were raised. Pots were stirred.

How-to-be-a-Jew rules unfolded in no particular order. The book of Leviticus was nothing but prohibitions: Don't murder. Don't eat a camel. Don't consider your menstrual period over until you've burned a lamb to make yourself clean. Report all rashes to Aaron the Priest or one of his sons. The Talmud was like a law textbook written by the most obsessive student in the class, with commentaries by all the other studious geeks. Who pays damages when one person's improperly tethered cow wanders onto another person's land, falls into a hole, and dies? Rabbi Baskin, who taught the first hour, once mentioned that the highest mitzvah is preparing the dead for burial, because they can't say thank you. Ellen Diesenhof, who taught the second, introduced us to *Yetzer Hara,* the Evil Inclination, which is part of our basic duality—black balancing white. It was nothing like my concept of Satan. You couldn't scrub it away or have it exorcised. No one *didn't* deal with *Yetzer Hara.* It came in the form of unethical ideas, disguised itself as your mother, appeared in print and on TV. I recognized *Yetzer Hara* immediately as the voice that says *If one jolt of heroin feels good, it follows logically that two would be twice as good.* You have to argue with it, and sometimes you have to accept it.

I could picture *Yetzer Hara.* The older, grizzled Kris Kristofferson could play him in the movie. I saw him hanging out in a diner in the mountains, charming and unassuming, so that everyone trusted him, told him their troubles, even ended up sleeping with him. Maybe he played guitar at the local bar and dealt a little hashish out of his pick-up truck. Often, you were glad to see him, but it was important to remember that he was toying coldly with humanity and that he was a bad, bad man.

Armed with unrelated snippets of Melton Judaism, I decided to become serious. Eric and I would learn Hebrew together, keep a strict Shabbat, go to every service, buy tickets to Israel. Keeping kosher sounded hard, but I thought we could do it if we all just pulled together.

Eric listened to this plan politely. Then he said no. No, he would not sign up. No, he would not fork over all his Friday nights—perhaps he might want to play in a dodgeball tournament or go out for tapas, driving a motor vehicle. No, he wouldn't give up cheeseburgers. No, he wouldn't take a two-week break from sex each month. No, no, no.

He said I was sounding a little cultish. I was furious. How could you immerse yourself in religion without following some of the rules, at least? I was no joiner, yet I began to feel aimless at being so unjoined.

"But how will we get closer to God?" I actually asked him, during an argument in the San Diego airport.

"I don't know. We'll just have to see what happens."

"Fine," I said. "We'll just be moderate Jews. Great. We'll find a way to slot it into our schedule."

There was no room in our schedule, and he knew it. Jenny and I were trying to take care of my father, whose type 2 diabetes had suddenly caught up with him. He was in and out of the hospital having plaque reamed from his arteries, his feet were covered with open wounds, and the doctors had discovered an aneurysm. Then his kidneys shut down. Dialysis was now his lifeline, three times a week. We wished he had managed to keep a wife.

One thing he still had was time to talk. I carried armloads of his photographs to the dialysis center, held them up one by one, and asked him to tell me the stories. They were all mixed up—he'd dumped his entire snapshot oeuvre into the army duffel bag he kept in his closet. We went from fighter pilot school (1956) to his first girlfriend (1944) to the Grand Canyon (1974), and sometimes he'd lose interest in the visuals and start stories that seemed unlikely to end, but I wrote them down anyway, because it made him feel famous. Anyway, I had an ulterior motive.

If I wore him down, I thought, if I worked my way through the layers of memories, I might get to something specifically Jewish. But every time I got close, he turned back toward the familiar.

"So, Dad. We're Jewish, and—"

"Did I ever tell you I knew Frank Sinatra?"

"Yes. He called you 'Chops.' So anyway, we're Jewish—"

"Yeah, and when my grandmother died, they had one of those ridiculous Jewish funerals and it was terrible, and Cookie and I started laughing and couldn't stop. We got kicked out of our own grandmother's funeral. So, what else? Did I ever tell you about that time I flew down to Havana with Bob and Sam and saw El Superman?"

He had, but I always liked that story. Also, I had stopped caring about whether or not it was true. I had brought my father a turkey sandwich with Russian dressing and coleslaw—meat and milk in one of their finest combos—but he'd been too sick to pay much attention to it. I ate it myself during the Cuba story. Finally, there came a pause.

"All right, then," I said. "Our family is *not* Jewish. We've always been agnostic."

"Not agnostic," he said. "Atheist. An atheist *knows* there's no God, and that's what I am. Your sister Jenny is, too. She's with me on this. To me, it all rests on science and proof. But you have to ask: How far back in the family does that go?"

"How far back does that go?"

"Well, to your great-grandfather. He was a rabbi, and no one liked him. I keep telling you no one else in the family believes that crap. No matter what their names sounded like—Gershwin, Stern, Zimbalist, all those guys—no one was acting Jewish. They were all just trying to survive. Did I tell you I met Katharine Hepburn in our hallway when I was a little boy?"

My grandfather was Katharine Hepburn's vocal coach for a time. You can be Jewish, my father was telling me, but please, not one of those overly-Jewish Jews. If you have to mess with religion, be a Katharine Hepburn kind of Jew!

"She wasn't Jewish at all," I pointed out.

"Well, but if she was. Better to be more like her, and less like those awful Dinnersteins."

I was a teenager when we met the awful Dinnersteins on a ski trip arranged by our new stepmother, Kris, who was fifteen years younger than Dad. She had young, fit friends who shared vacation houses. The big draw was Kris's famous Swedish friend Gunilla Knudsen, who had made a notorious TV commercial in which she purred, "Take it off, take it off, take it aaaaaalllll off—with Noxzema Medicated Cream." She appeared on talk shows and had even written a healthy Swedish beauty cookbook.

Gunilla and her husband, Per, were the first truly sexy adults I'd ever met. At fourteen, I lived to babysit for them. As soon as their baby was asleep, I'd wander around their apartment pretending to be them—imagining myself in Gunilla's shorty bathrobe with the Swedish flag on the pocket, or in her silver bikini bottom. (I never saw her wear the top.) Per was such an utter Nordic god that I couldn't speak when he was in the room. Naturally, they were both excellent skiers.

Into this white-blond world came the Dinnersteins. Gunilla had met them somewhere and decided to make them part of her gang. They were friendly, but absolutely awful, according to my father. They had grating outer-borough accents. The Dinnerstein boys reached for food at the table and had their hands slapped by Mrs. Dinnerstein, with her long, fake fingernails. And they referred to smoked salmon, a food sacred to my father, as "Novy." As in, "Wouldja pass the Novy?"

My father was insulted by the presence of the Dinnersteins, who came from the same appalling tribe as his dentist, Sid Silver. Sid was always inviting my Dad to go sailing, but he captained a boat known as the Bay Gull, and was therefore, my father said, an embarrassment to yachting.

"Jesus, remember them?" he said, laid out in his dialysis chair. "Horrible people."

I wondered if my father had always been such a snob. When I was a kid, his friends had always come from everywhere. True, he was fascinated by rich people, but only because they had money, which, in his view, existed for the purpose of instant gratification. He never understood why the rich didn't use this important tool more often and more enthusiastically. His station in life, whatever that was, meant nothing to him, and he had nothing against any minority I could think of. Except, possibly, those very Jewish Jews. They made him flinch.

"So Dad," I asked. "Is there something embarrassing about Jews in general?"

"This is a trap, a conversation like this. But okay, there is. Yes. They've always embarrassed me. When I was young, I was embarrassed by my grandfather. He was always following me around, even on the subway, and he spoke with a very heavy accent, and he brought hardboiled eggs and calves' foot jelly along, and ate them in public. And he called me Blairchik. I loved him, but I tried to distance myself from him. It sounds terrible, but I was embarrassed. Hell, I was embarrassed I didn't have a simple American name."

It wasn't just the old-country Jews, either, he said. The world was full of pushy people who looked and acted Jewish and didn't care. As a nightlife writer in the fifties, he went on a press junket to Miami and was horrified.

"They behaved like their own clichés," he said, "these people who gathered just to eat and eat and eat at the hotel buffets. And in the Catskills it was even worse—the women, even on a nice warm day, as long as it was winter, wearing mink coats and ski boots even though you knew they'd never ski a day in their lives. It was in terrible taste."

The next time I went to dialysis, Dad was ready for me. "You always want to talk about this Jewish stuff," he said. "Well, I finally thought of something."

"And?"

"Food. Food is important to a Jew. The *goyim,* we thought, didn't really care about food. Their tastes were, you know, really *goyish.* Boiled dinners and that kind of thing, but what am I saying? Is that fair? All I know is, in any Jewish refrigerator, you would find something to eat."

"What was in those other refrigerators?"

"The *goyim?* Oh, boy. My dad used to give piano lessons at an estate on Long Island. These people were filthy rich. One time I went with him, and we spent the night, and at midnight we went down to the kitchen to raid the WASP refrigerator, and there was nothing in it but some cocktail onions and ginger ale. And this was a beautiful, big refrigerator, like a Sub-Zero, but before they'd been invented. To us, this seemed very strange."

I'd heard this story before, too, but now it had gained a nearly Sub-Zero refrigerator and carried a Jewish subtext. This in itself was Jewish, because what do Jews do but repeat the same stories over and over again, looking for something new?

My twenty-seven-year-old half-sister, Marina, came home from San Francisco during our second round of High Holy Days. Fifteen years younger than me and raised by my father and Kris, who were dedicated to cooking, she loved the idea of a holiday that centers around a feast. For Rosh Hashanah, I made challah in the shape of a circle, and Marina made everything else—including mojito Jell-O shots. After dinner, she said she would come to the synagogue with us.

"Why?" I asked. "I thought you were, you know, like Dad."

"Well, yeah. I grew up with that whole bitter, bothered atheist thing about only weak people believing in God, how it's a crutch," she said. "And at high school, the religious youth group kids were the biggest hoodlums I ever met. But I've had my moments of believing in something. The closest was at Sacré Coeur in Paris. It was a big religious scene with a big white glowing Jesus, and I was really, really moved. I thought somehow it would make it easier to believe in something, to be embraced by that big Jesus, that you could go to a place like this when things got really bad."

Jesus, Moses, Allah—it was all the same to her. But now that my family had joined a synagogue, she'd decided to read up on Jewish ritual. "I love the whole idea of the seder," she said. "It's food representing history. All my Catholic friends get is a wafer and a cup of wine."

I don't know how impressed she was by the service. It was long, long, long and Rabbi Baskin's sermon consisted mostly of encouraging us to vote for Al Gore, because he was running with Joseph Lieberman, a Jew. But Coco, who had started attending Jewish summer camp, knew all the songs and chants, just as I had hoped.

"You're lucky," Marina said when it was over. "You have this whole community of people not related to each other or even good friends, but they're all interested, no one looks bored, and everyone seems very moved even though they've seen it before."

Eric and I fasted for the first time that Yom Kippur. It made me feel light and efficient, then tired and discouraged. I thought about people who did the same thing most days, and not by choice. Which was the whole point, as it is in so many religions—to relate to people engaged in a brutal daily struggle with hunger. But this was uniquely Jewish, too. It didn't seem to involve breaking our attachment to the desire for food, or proving our self-discipline. Fasting was a way to focus on atonement. And when it was time to eat, we went to a Mexican place. The first margarita packed such a magnificent punch that we decided to make it a yearly tradition. There. We had a tradition of our own!

A year later, Rosh Hashanah was beginning to seem familiar. Our children missed a day of school other kids didn't. The sanctuary required folding chairs. The *oneg* after services featured herring and smoked salmon. And we sang "Avinu Malkenu," the heart-wrenching song that prepares us to atone on Yom Kippur, and I cried, as usual. But this year we also sang "God Bless America," Rabbi Baskin wore an American flag tie, and the ritual committee had asked for "personal reflections" that might somehow add to the day. Only three weeks had passed since 9/11. I asked to be a personal reflector, and was approved. My hands shook so hard I could barely hold my pages.

I recalled a scene from Laura Ingalls Wilder's *The Long Winter,* in which she and Pa discover a muskrat house in autumn. Its walls are very thick. This, Pa says, means the coming winter will be long and vicious.

"Pa, how can the muskrats know?" she asked.

"I don't know how they know," Pa said, "but they do. God tells them, somehow, I suppose."

"Then why doesn't God tell us?" Laura wanted to know.

"Because," said Pa, "we're not animals. We're humans, and, like it says in the Declaration of Independence, God created us free. That means we got to take care of ourselves."

Laura said faintly, "I thought God takes care of us."

"He does," Pa said, "so far as we do what's right. And He gives us a conscience and brains to know what's right. But He leaves it to us to do as we please. That's the difference between us and everything else in creation."

"Can't muskrats do what they please?" Laura asked, amazed.

"No," said Pa. "I don't know why they can't but you can see they can't."

And then I speculated on the responsibilities that come with free will.

I sat back down feeling as if a switch had been thrown inside me. Occasionally, when I played piano on a stage, there was a wonderful gig with a sound system that worked so that people could hear, and even listen to, my lyrics. *This is just the beginning,* I'd think. *Now a record company will sign me and I'll play for bigger, politer audiences. And maybe I'll meet Willie Dixon.* Cycles of success and failure being what they are, my thoughts always turned out to have been a bunch of hooey.

But after addressing the congregation, I understood why a person would want to be a rabbi or a minister. It was refreshing to tell your version of the truth to people who actually listened. They weren't drunk. They weren't trying desperately to fall in love. My speech wouldn't change the course of my life, but it was an interesting thing to have done and would lead to more interesting conversations than I had had over herring thus far. I thought I'd like to do it again.

Then it was Christmas, and we embarked on the complicated lottery system Eric's family uses to keep each family from going broke. Names are drawn so that each adult only has to buy one present. Eric's sister, Karen, keeps track, and she e-mailed us when the results were in.

"Okay, you buy for Jill and Robin buys for Dan," she wrote. "Ho ho ho, or whatever your guy says."

So it was official. Our guy was the Chanukah guy. As a holiday, it was minor, but absorbing—especially the parts about Judah Maccabee, a sort of Jewish Green Beret who succeeded despite the odds. We had a lot of other guys in the family—an assortment of Catholics, Lutherans, and atheists—and everyone was used to the mix.

We spun some dreidl and ate some *gelt*. I experimented with low-fat, baked latkes. They were awful, and I went back to deep-frying, which filled the house with a deep-fried smell. In the beginning, I had regretted the loss of Christmas, which had had its magical points. I wondered if my kids would feel cheated, but then again, they weren't those kind of kids. Also, we had acquired another two menorahs, and on nights when the sun set at 4:30 P.M. they worked exactly as intended, shedding light. A little more of it every year.

I LEARNED TO make quilts the year Coco studied for her bat mitzvah. Both of us did a lot of sitting around in religious classes that year—a scholarly Jewish tradition if there ever was one. Needing something to do with my hands, I was inspired by Joanne Greenberg, who never went anywhere without a bag full of quilt pieces, needles, thread, and a long, vicious pair of scissors she called her "pigsticker." "A lady should always carry one," she said.

I bought a bag of fabric scraps—called "fat quarters" by those who knew—and began to sew shapes together. In a few weeks, I had made an insipid-looking thing the size of a place mat.

"It's too matchy-matchy," the old ladies at the fabric counter said. "Don't think about colors. Just let them happen."

"Right," said Joanne. "Also, I think a quilt should be used, not hung on a wall. The idea of an *art quilt* does not appeal to me."

That was why the quilt on the wall of the Methodist Church social hall didn't work. It *was* matchy-matchy, dusty rose and lavender, and all it did was sit. In an obnoxious mood, it was possible to compare our religion with the Methodists', using the same terminology. They were matchy-matchy—we were a bunch of eccentrics. I started over with quilting and this time my designs came to me in dreams. I took requests, but wouldn't even listen to anyone's color scheme ideas. They got what they got.

"Boy," said my friends, when they saw me sewing, "you don't seem like the type."

And I never did think I'd sit quietly sewing during a religious instruction class. Go figure.

Coco and the other twelve-year-olds were expected to train with Joanne every other Tuesday. (On alternate weeks, they had open-ended conversations about Jewish philosophy and practice with Phil Zeitler, an agnostic pediatrician who later became our synagogue president.) Since the kids' bat and bar mitzvahs were scattered all over the calendar, the class was a work in progress with no beginning or end. The kids came and went, got older, had their celebrations and moved on.

They began as a handful of preteenagers trying hard not to look stupid, sitting in a clump on the white sheepskin covered floor. Joanne didn't start out with trust-building exercises or games designed to help everyone remember everyone else's name.

"Somebody sing something for me," she said. Silence. This didn't seem to surprise her. "Sing anything. 'Happy Birthday to You.' 'Comet.' You know 'Comet,' don't you? 'Comet—it's made of gas-o-leen. Comet. It makes your teeth turn green . . .'" The room remained silent. Finally, Coco sang a few bars of "Happy Birthday" without moving her gaze from the floor. She sang it in a low mumble, which was odd, since whenever I walked by her room, she was belting out Frank Sinatra tunes. Another kid tried something by Eminem, which technically didn't involve singing. Joanne didn't look discouraged.

"What you're about to do is impossible," she told them. "If you don't want to do it, get out now, for God's sake." Of course, *that* was impossible, too. Most of the parents had already alerted their extended families in New Jersey, rented halls, and hired videographers and caterers, as if the upcoming bar and bat mitzvahs weren't much different from weddings, and maybe they weren't. Because Coco had no Jewish family, we didn't have to worry about all that. The bat mitzvah would be her academic exercise, performed in a new dress—the only part I knew for certain she was looking forward to.

Jews are supposed to read the entire Torah—the five books of Moses, from Genesis through Deuteronomy—every year. Simchat Torah, a holiday that comes right after Sukkot during the crowded fall schedule of Jewish holidays, simultaneously celebrates the end of one year's Torah reading and the beginning of the next. It's a geeky, studious holiday in which Jews celebrate the fact that their homework never ends. But it's also a raucous, physical holiday in which Jews dance around the sanctuary seven times and the congregation unrolls the scroll around the perimeter of the room, holding it up for the children to see.

Each weekly portion is followed by a *haftarah*—a reading from the Prophets. (The custom dates back to an ancient Greek time when Jews were under the rule of Antiochus and weren't allowed to read Torah at all.) The *haftarah* usually corresponds loosely with the week's general theme. Some Deuteronomy Torah portions, for instance, are so crammed with plagues and miseries that they're followed by a *"haftarah* of consolation," which is supposed to refer to the destruction of the temple, but is also intended to cheer the reader up.

Coco's ceremony was set for August 16, which meant she'd be reading from Deuteronomy and Isaiah. Torah portions are known by their first word, in Coco's case *"Eikev,"* which means "Obey"—interesting, in light of the way she approached homework. When she didn't feel like doing it, she had her reasons: the teacher hadn't assigned it in time, she misunderstood, she felt a little sick to her stomach. Long-term assignments—science projects, books with multiple chapters—were most daunting. I agreed with Joanne: The long-term assignment she'd decided to undertake was probably impossible. I loved Coco in the way you always love an oldest child, and she was very smart, but this yearlong process wouldn't play to her strengths. Not only that,

I'd never be able to check her progress, because what did I know from Hebrew chanting?

There didn't seem to be any organized curriculum, other than the "this is impossible" speech, but there was plenty of accountability. At each class, one or two kids were selected to sing their portions, or as much as they knew of them. When they sounded good—part of which was being able to sing over the noise of Joanne's loud and antiquated answering machine—or answered a Talmudic question thoughtfully, she handed them a realistic-looking plastic fly. For the first three months, Coco didn't get a single bug. She began to understand the Ten Commandments, but her Torah portion, it turned out, was a mess. At first, we thought it was indulgent when the other kids' parents hired Hebrew tutors, but Coco begged, and we gave in.

Ellen Diesenhof charged forty bucks per hour. She had recently moved from New Jersey to Evergreen and had, as Joanne said, forgotten more about Judaism than the rest of us would ever learn. Apparently, Ellen and Coco had already met at Hebrew school. Ellen said she would very much enjoy teaching Coco, and would charge us . . . well, she had to think about it. She must have concluded—accurately—that we were on the lower end of our synagogue's wage scale. The next day she called back and offered her services for nothing.

I began dropping Coco off at Ellen's house after school, and when I came back, they'd be eating Oreos, drinking Diet Coke, and discussing the human condition like two old ladies at the JCC, as if no work had been done at all. But I was wrong about that. Ellen was full of positive reinforcement, but was clear about exactly how much work would be done between tutoring sessions. The few times Coco missed the mark, she was silent on the ride home. I never heard a single instance of "Ellen said I had to do this, but she didn't give me time" or "Ellen plays favorites." As far as I could tell, Ellen was pleasant, tough, and fair, and something about her brought Coco into line.

Whenever I joined them at the kitchen table, Ellen dragged me into the conversation, trying to graft some knowledge onto me.

"What other religion tells you sex on the Sabbath is a mitzvah?" she asked me one Friday afternoon before sundown.

"None," I said, after thinking it over.

"Right," said Ellen. "I'm proud of you, sweetie. You're really picking this up."

"I guess I'd like to be a good Jew," I said. "If there is such a thing."

"There certainly is," Ellen said firmly. "I've been a Jew all my life and I always wanted to be, because I bought into the idea that we were better and special, that the goyim were fine, but we were just a little bit better. We didn't drink like them, we were brighter and more compassionate. Jews, they told me, don't womanize. They don't abandon their partners, they're honest and moral. It took me a long time to realize that Meyer Lansky was also a Jew, but by that time, it didn't matter. If this was an ideal, I was proud to be part of it."

Ellen and her husband, Marty, had met in yeshiva elementary school and cemented their courtship at a Hebrew-language summer camp. Marty considered himself a religious agnostic but still appeared to be an involved and charitable Jew, so knowledgeable that he had no trouble running services whenever Rabbi Baskin couldn't.

"I thought this synagogue was very strange at first," Ellen remembered. "Our first service seemed awfully loose. The rabbi's kids were running all over the place—*everyone's* kids were running all over. I know this sounds terrible, but in the end we joined because I thought they needed us."

She had her own no-nonsense ideas of how to raise Jewish kids, and over the course of the year I learned some of them. Here's what you tell them when they want to play in a soccer match on Rosh Hashanah: *Forget it.* Here's why it made sense to keep a strictly kosher kitchen, with separate dishes for milk and meat, but allow yourself to eat bacon in the outside world:

"You want to know why? I'll tell you why," she said. "Shrimp and bacon are delicious. You eat them, nothing happens. You don't fall through the floor. My keeping a kosher home is nothing more than an effort to not make everything convenient and easy. I wanted my children raised knowing what kosher was. Immediate gratification? No. Just 'cause everyone else can do it? No."

It wasn't a bad grounding for a Jewish kid, who would always have to accept being part of a peculiar minority.

"A lot of these laws make sense when you think about them," Ellen said.

A lot of these laws came up at Joanne's.

"What does a Jew do when she hears an ambulance nearby?" was a typical question. "Does she pray that no one is hurt? Or dead?"

Yes? No? Anyone?

No. It's perhaps more Jewish to think, *Whatever happens there, I pray they can handle it.* Maybe God granted specific requests in biblical times, but these days he doesn't seem much inclined to let us suggest who lives, dies, or ends up in traction.

"Do you remember how different Jews are?" Joanne asked. "How we are not, for instance, Christians? Not believing in God? That's not a religious issue for us. Not knowing if there's heaven or hell—some say yes, some say no, but it's not a religious issue. Redemption? Who cares—not a religious issue, not a problem. But *I notice you didn't say hello to your father when you walked into the room*—that's a religious issue."

So, honor your parents. "But what if your mother is an axe murderer? Do you have to be wonderful to her? I don't think so. But what if she's a homeless ax murderer? Do you have to pay her rent and make sure she gets enough to eat, even if you don't bring over the groceries yourself? Well, probably."

She left us with that thought.

The next time I saw my father, he was in the hospital having a plaque-filled artery reamed out. There had been at least a half dozen chest pain episodes in the past few weeks, and he was popping nitroglycerine like candy. He'd been saying he was on the verge of a heart attack ever since I could remember—it was his stock excuse for avoiding vigorous tennis matches and boring social functions—but I thought maybe he meant it this time.

We sat in a curtained-off waiting room, waiting for the procedure to begin. A woman was moaning on the other side of the fabric. It sounded like "hell, hell, hell," but could have been "help."

"Jesus, Rob," Dad said. "Did you ever think I'd end up like this?"

"Yes," I said, causing him to laugh hard enough to require another nitroglycerine pill. But had my comment counted as honoring my father? I asked if he needed anything.

"Nah," he said. "Just sit here with me."

I sat there all day, oddly calm as I handwrote that week's column, while the TV blasted *Oprah*. Dad came out of the anesthesia stoned and happy.

"I love you," he said, looking at me with watery eyes.

"I love you, too," I said.

"Do you think I'm going to croak?"

This was a question my mother never dared ask, even when she was clearly dying of cancer, because she was afraid of the answer. My father wasn't, but it made me a little nervous.

"We're all going to croak eventually," I said.

The admissions people were always trying to get him to sign documents defining which "extreme measures" he wanted taken should he end up on life support, but he wouldn't, even though he knew it would make things easier for his family. This sort of waffling was harder on my sister Marina than me. After all, she had to live with the guy.

She and her fiancé, Ryan, had moved home from San Francisco because Ryan, whose straightforward morals were distinctly un-Chotzinoff, had said it was the only right thing to do. He'd seen me and Jenny trying to ride herd on the doctor appointments, medication lists, and midnight ambulance rides. They hadn't stopped. They were getting worse.

At first, Marina had a hazy picture of what it would be like to live with Dad. She'd settle him with the paper in the morning, go to yoga, come home, and make him a cup of tea. She'd ease his final days and he'd be grateful. That lasted about a week. Then they argued, an activity Dad enjoyed a lot more than Marina did. Dad, for instance, grew bored with his false teeth and ordered that all his food be pureed. Marina pureed, but seethed, especially when she had to watch him gum his meals. They sat upstairs, in adjoining rooms, writing Chotzinovian e-mails to each other until they settled down, which usually happened because of Ryan.

"Blair, I don't think you really meant to say that to Marina, did you?"

"Marina, you want a beer?"

Once in a very great while, Marina and Ryan fought with each other, which kept Dad on the edge of his seat, astonishingly alert to the gossip unfolding *under his own roof!*

"I want to be kept alive if there's any chance at all," he explained. "I *like* to live."

He didn't mind filling out the more philosophical statement known as the Five Wishes. Here are the central statements my father made so that they would live on after he died:

1. More is better.
2. Saran Wrap is good.
3. Things change.
4. I love my daughters.

There was no number five.

ONE DAY, SIX months after she'd started the Joanne classes, Coco suddenly began to sing in Hebrew. The other kids used a singsong mumble and that was perfectly acceptable—it was the voice their fathers had used at *their* bar mitzvahs. But Coco had listened to the tape Joanne made her, and was actually following the mysterious squiggly marks above and below the Hebrew text, known as trope marks. When she sang, the room got very quiet. It appeared she *was* studying. She earned her fly.

Every other week, I absorbed a little more of Joanne. She didn't own a sewing machine—she had nothing against them, but they were too noisy to use while watching TV. She made her own shoelaces using a technique she'd learned from a costumed interpreter at Plimoth Colony. Albert had built her a cinder-block root cellar now so crammed with homemade pickles, jam, wine, and beeswax candles that you could survive a famine there and have a few drinks while you were at it.

One night after class, she took me into her bedroom to show me some of the quilts I hadn't seen. She had several prayer shawls in there, too. I touched their fringes and realized it was time to get one for Coco.

"What about you, Moonbeam?" Joanne suddenly asked. "When are you going to have your bat mitzvah?"

Never? (Moonbeam?)

Well, not now. This is Coco's year. How Joan Crawford to over-shadow her with a surge of competitive religious fervor—it would take the role of inappropriate mom to new heights.

"I'm not too old?" I asked.

~ 113 ~

"Nope. We've had several adult b'nai mitzvoth. They were private occasions, not even held in the synagogue. We set the pace ourselves, but we also sent an announcement to the world: 'I didn't get to do this when I was thirteen, and now that I have control, this is what I choose.' These things can be very moving."

"Did you have a bat mitzvah?"

"No," she said, "but I never went to Morocco, either."

I couldn't stop thinking about it. What would it mean to become an adult when I already was one?

ONE WINTER DAY, Marina called to inform me that she and Ryan were burnt out. I agreed to spell them for a few hours. Later that afternoon, I found myself closer to an adult diaper than I ever thought I'd be, unless that diaper was my own. The house was unbearably stuffy; the hands on the clock seemed to have gone on strike. *I agreed to honor my father,* I thought, *but this is crossing the line.* These are the things we're never supposed to mention—there's such a loss of dignity for the diaper wearer. But my father didn't seem to care about the missing boundaries and he certainly didn't want strangers taking care of him.

Over amaretto sours, Marina and I considered his wishes and then vetoed them. We hired Nurse Steve, a man in his fifties who'd retired from a career with the utilities company, and sent him up the stairs to deal with Dad. Within weeks, he was walking the dog, frying the eggs, and half-carrying my father up and down stairs. He arranged Medicaid rides to and from dialysis, and a rusty station wagon manned by Russian immigrants began turning up in the alley. The Russians loved my father and took to bringing him homemade blini with sour cream and little Slavic pastries.

But Dad was incensed. He'd always been the kind of person who wouldn't carpool to a party, for fear of not being able to escape when he wanted to. So he pulled his trump card—magical thinking. He asked his old friend Sam for a lump of cash and bought himself a brand-new Chevrolet Suburban. It sat in his garage emitting drive vibes and causing my father to hope and hope, despite the fact that his three daughters had formed a cartel to keep him from ever driving again. His feet were numb—they could slip all over the brake and accelerator and cause dramatic damage. Not just to him, either. When we shut off all his wheedling, he became petulant and refused to speak to us. He put all his efforts into the magic car, but nothing happened. He was too weak to open the driver's side door, let alone crank over the engine.

So he started speaking to us again, in order to entertain himself by stirring the pot.

For my express benefit, he started a conversation about my sister Jenny, who had recently become a very successful wine writer.

"She's damn well as good a writer as you are," he said conversationally, "and she's only been doing it for a few years. You, you've been doing it about thirty years now, right? How do you explain her incredible talent?"

"She's very talented," I agreed. "Very funny, too." But I seethed with rivalry. I hadn't felt this way since the violent fights Jenny and I used to have when we were eight and nine. We certainly tried to hurt each other. I was quite a bit heavier, but she was wiry and quick, like a squirrel. You had to admire Dad's skill. After forty years, he had me wound up. I was dying to sneak into Jenny's house and deface her stuffed animals, if she still had any.

THE OTHER B'NOT mitzvah parents recommended the book *Putting God on the Guest List*. It explained the novel concept of re-membering that the service was a spiritual occasion—much more important than the caterer, the rented hall, the DJ. The DJ? Why on earth did we need a DJ?

But as Coco's friends were called to the Torah one after an-other, and Coco went to their parties, I learned that a DJ was just the beginning. There were also inflatable guitars, commemorative baseball caps, and dayglow necklaces. The parties were held at country clubs and event centers. All those things sounded shal-low and indulgent—"What's next," Ellen asked, "riding an ele-phant into Yankee Stadium?"—but when I finally went to my first bat mitzvah, I cried through the entire thing. A particularly frivo-lous friend of Coco's—I called her That Squeaker—stood calmly on the bimah, wrapped in a prayer shawl, and ran the entire ser-vice. I was stunned by how fast a squeaky girl could grow up.

As Coco's day approached, Rabbi Baskin asked us to bring her to his study to talk over her speech. He had moved away from our town into a high-end Denver suburb, and the sheer square footage of his new house intimidated us. His office was lined with books, not just in Hebrew and English, but Arabic and Aramaic.

Coco had a question: How was she supposed to account for God's behavior in her Torah portion? If the Jews acted right, they'd be rewarded with perfect land and good crops forever: "... For the Lord your God is bringing you into a good land, a land with streams and springs and fountains ... a land of wheat and barley ... of olive trees and honey ..." But if they didn't, he'd smite them with a laundry list of horrible fates: "I warn you this day that you shall certainly perish ... "

"Not all Jews are bad," she pointed out, "and they haven't gotten all that good stuff."

Rabbi Baskin leaned back in his chair thoughtfully. "There are many things we don't understand," he said, "and many things we never thought could happen before they did. A hundred years ago, did we think it was possible that a man could stand on the moon?"

Coco wasn't impressed. She had started to feel territorial about her Torah portion and wasn't about to settle for vague optimism. *Eikev* contained the whole of the *Ve'ahavta,* a prayer Jews say at every service. It tells them when and how to be public Jews—to mark their doorposts, their heads and forearms, to teach their children, and to think of these things when they lie down and when they rise. It was perfect for Coco at this particular time in her life. She didn't care who knew she was Jewish. The idea of marking doorposts and teaching children was right up her alley.

We moved on to logistics. The Chain of Generations, for instance: the part of the service in which Coco's grandparents hand the Torah to her parents, her parents pass it on to her and she holds it while singing the *Shema*—the central Jewish prayer that translates as "Hear, O Israel, God is One." (Or, as our new rabbi likes to say: "Listen, you God Wrestlers, wrestle with this: God is One.") It was time to drum up a pair of appropriate grandparents, because you couldn't be part of the chain unless you called yourself a Jew.

Eric's mother, Betsy, decided she could call herself a Jew. While she admired Jesus, she didn't really believe he was immortal, or even the son of God.

I excused my father from the Chain. I knew it would make him uncomfortable, and besides, he'd been so sick. He didn't even have to go to the ceremony if he didn't want to, and if he did, Nurse Steve could take him home after the first hour. A grandfather wasn't absolutely necessary, and I knew he didn't want to stand up in person and call himself a Jew, and if he just wanted to ponder it—

"Shut up a second," he said. "I thought about it, already. I'll do it."

We rented a charming, if slightly damp, community center for the party, and found Moses, a Hispanic DJ who agreed to be known as DJ Moish for the evening. My sisters, who may have worked this out in advance, acted like any other Jewish aunts. Jenny took Coco shopping for not one but two purple dresses— one for the ceremony, one for the afterparty—and she rustled up a few cases of wine. Marina and Ryan developed and cooked a fancy yet kosher dinner and served it, even though Marina had had an emergency appendectomy two days before the service. We pulled together a guest list, heavy on *goyim*.

The service was blurry for me, almost a mirage. Coco and I got to the synagogue fifteen minutes early, a time when traditional parents order the videographer around and have still photos taken with the congratulatory rabbi, as if the event had already occurred. Coco went over her speech one last time and admired the acrylic fingernails she'd paid for with her own money—not an un-Jewish accessory, when you think about it. I tried to take a few pictures with my new camera, but the automatic flash made her blink. Gus sat down in the front row in a crisp pink dress. She was five, and I wondered how much of the three-hour service she'd be able to tolerate. Coco's middle-school friends began to file in, some of them in slinky prom dresses. The synagogue had found us a cantor—Alyssa Stanton, the first black female in history to pursue that job. She'd come in from Hebrew Union College in Cincinnati, where she was studying to be the country's first black, female rabbi.

"I'd love to write your story," I said.

She said, understandably, that media attention had left her exhausted.

Ludwig showed up with his wife and sixteen-year-old stepdaughter. Nurse Steve walked my father down the aisle. Ellen Diesenhof huddled with Coco, going over the portion one last time. Joanne greeted me with: "You know what doesn't suck? Idi Amin died today!"

Looking around the synagogue, I saw that I had gradually gotten to know most of the Jews. I rode bikes with them, hung out in the hall at Hebrew school, and attended seminars for dummies, such as Chanukah 101. Almost every one of them had asked what they could do to help, and I realized that no one would be put off by a party in a moldy, log-cabin community center, never mind how many country clubs they'd been to.

The service rolled slowly toward the Chain of Generations. We got my father up to the bimah, where he stood, swaying a little, on his foam diabetic shoes. It turned out the "passing" of the Torah was more of a metaphor—instead of letting us hold it, Rabbi Baskin tapped us with it in passing, except my father, whom he jabbed by mistake. My father grimaced. He didn't like Rabbi Baskin. They had met once, at Saint Luke's Hospital. For some unaccountable reason, Dad filled in the "Faith" blank on his hospital admission with the word "Jewish." Naturally, the Jewish Community Chaplain showed up.

"Your father is charming," Rabbi Baskin reported. "And what a sense of humor! Oy va-voy!"

"Your rabbi wears the yarmulke and everything," my father complained. "*Never* send him here again."

"Dad had a great time with your rabbi," Jenny said. "He told us all about it."

"Okay, he was a perfectly nice man," my father admitted, "but don't send him here again."

That wasn't because Dad didn't think he'd be in the hospital again. We all knew he would. Or because he didn't like visitors—he did, especially visitors bearing Chinese takeout. It wasn't because religious leaders intimidated him. He used to love drinking with a Jesuit priest. The problem he had, of course, was with Jews, and even then, if Henny Youngman had shown up, it would have been great. But a rabbi? He had a bone to pick, as he would say, with such a person. It didn't help that one of the first questions Rabbi Baskin asked was when, exactly, he had given up his Jewish faith.

"Never!" I could hear my father exploding. "I am an *atheist*, and don't you forget it."

This was probably what Rabbi Baskin meant when he referred to Dad's sense of humor, even though my Dad had been deadly serious. It was probably what my Dad meant when he cited the yarmulke "and everything."

In any case, they recognized each other, and then the Rabbi stabbed him in the chest. For the first time, my father was touched—hard—by the Torah. He gave me a *rescue me* look, but I turned away. I concentrated on Coco.

She was shimmering. The sun coming in through the sanctuary windows picked out the iridescent purple in her dress and the amethysts in her ears. Suddenly, she looked about twenty-six years old, the kind of young woman raised among Greek shipping tycoons and Mediterranean soirees, who knew how to use silverware from the outside in, who had already had her first glass of champagne.

It was time for one of my assigned mom roles, to carry the Torah around the congregation so that people could touch it with their prayer books. The klezmer band began to play, and I found myself practically running through the crowd. It was supposed to be a social procession—the rabbi and I would greet the people, shake hands, kiss cheeks. But all I did was smile and jog past, feeling very light.

I sat back down and watched as Coco chanted from the Torah in her amazing new voice. I watched Eric read the words he'd prepared, and was surprised to see he was crying.

"She taught me how Bach should sound played on a cello," he said. "She taught me what to do when a four-year-old won't stop screaming."

Coco's father looked stunned. He was crying, too, and so was Susan, who cleans our house, Ada, who drives the school bus, my sick father, and Coco herself, but even while doing that, she seemed at ease.

That night we partied at the Indian Hills community center with DJ Moish, who played the disco music I hated in the 1970s and now had occasion to hate again, if I had the power to hate anything on that day, which I didn't. My father sat outside under the trees and complained about the noise, but when Coco came out to see him, he got teary all over again and told her how impressed he was.

"And I was," he said to me after she was gone. "All that chanting, even if it *was* in a dead language. All the work that must have gone into it."

"And for what?" I prompted.

"No, I know for what. Don't be a wiseapple."

Inside, Coco danced alone to the strains of "I've Got the World on a String," holding her favorite bat mitzvah present—a framed poster of Frank Sinatra—and wearing a paper crown. She was the same girl who had road-tripped all over the West with me during my single years, when we slept in the same bed even though the experts advised against it. The girl who got interested in beavers and dragged me to wildlife refuges and begged me to hold a Beaver Theme Party for her fifth birthday, which I did, despite all the snickers. The same girl who shook her booty to any music, cried when I read *Little Big Man* aloud, who could talk to people about themselves when she was supposedly too young to think about anyone but herself. Whose mitzvah project had been to have conversations with Alzheimer's patients. Who wasn't afraid of hospitals, illness, or death. Who had already started arguing with me regularly, even though she had yet to enter high school. Who still played with dolls but was interested in a certain boy. A shimmery purple girl in a crown.

Such pure happiness filled me that I now thought DJ Moish had been worth every penny. He was part of the structure Coco had built for herself, doing one tough thing after another until she earned the prize. Not for nothing do people use the word "transformation" to describe a bat mitzvah.

SOME KIDS BACK off from religion after their bnai mitzvoth. Coco didn't. She'd impressed all the old synagogue ladies, was teaching Hebrew school, and even talked of becoming a rabbi. Why would she turn her back on all the acclaim? For the moment, she was an über-Jew.

Sometimes I looked forward to the time when I could say, "My daughter, the *rabbi*, has an interesting perspective on that." When I wasn't proud, though, I was a little disturbed.

"I think I'm probably more conservative than you," Coco said.

"Well, duh."

"I'm more *Orthodox* than you. I like Orthodox. I might marry an Orthodox guy and have a lot of kids and live in Brooklyn."

"*What???* Are you crazy? You'll be a woman. They won't let you do anything."

"Like what?"

"Go to college. I heard they think women should stay home with the kids. You don't get anywhere if you don't go to college."

"You didn't go to college," she pointed out. "At least the Orthodox have rules. You don't."

That was deflating. I didn't have Jewish rules of any kind.

Coco was probably in the middle of one of those understandable thirteen-year-old phases. At her age, I had a brief flirtation with gymnastics. (I was incredibly, almost hilariously, lousy at it.) But I thought it would be nice to think of God in Coco's literal way. *God made Adam and Eve. He opened the Sea of Reeds. He stuck out his superhero arm and caused calamities and miracles.* I'd accept all that if I didn't think it was hooey.

I believed in a metaphoric God, a force flowing through all things, a flavor I happened to taste. I'd also heard intriguing mentions of an intensely feminine Jewish God, a radiant "Sabbath bride" who appeared on Friday nights to inaugurate twenty-four hours of uncluttered rest. I hadn't seen her around, though.

My ignorance reminded me weirdly of the young Moses of the Torah. "Who the hell are you?"—or words to that effect—was the very first question he'd asked God-as-burning-bush. "I am that I am," God replied, or words to that effect. Was that a concrete answer? Hardly. Moses was still stuck in metaphor land, not knowing what, exactly, to do now that he was a real Jew. The rules and regs came later—not just ten, but 613 commandments—but in the beginning, it seemed, he was left to wonder, *Now what?*

That was the problem with belonging to a "post-denominational" synagogue, unaffiliated with any of the accepted Jewish sects. We didn't line up with anyone's operating instructions. We used a lot of Hebrew, wore prayer shawls, and sat through long services—as the more conservative congregations do—but we also had musical instruments, yoga classes, and a group of men who met to go snowboarding. The only part I related to instinctively was a prayer book written by the Reconstructionists, a group of Jews so questioning and argumentative that they didn't even have a formal position on whether or not God exists.

Mine was a blurry Judaism, and if I was going to have a bat mitzvah, vaguely Jewish thoughts bolstered by the occasional service wouldn't be enough. I would have to be some particular kind of Jew. So I decided to go out into the wide Jewish world and collect opinions. I wouldn't expect consensus—"Two Jews, five opinions," Rabbi Baskin liked to say—but I'd push for clarity.

Here was my big question: *What does a Jew need to know and do?*

"WHAT DOES A Jew need to know and do?" I asked Joanne Greenberg two weeks after Coco's bat mitzvah, as we chowed on Vietnamese.

"What *is* a Jew?" she countered. "Which parts make sense? Which don't?"

"Well, I like that I can think about all kinds of forbidden things. Like sometimes I think I invented God, not the other way round. But then, I don't like that it smacks of peasant superstition. My family rejects religion because there's no proof."

"Oh, so it's a matter of proof, is it?" she said. "If there's no God, how could there be the mitzvah of bees? How would anything get pollinated?"

"My father would explain that with science."

"Good for him. But there's more than one way to explain things. I'll tell you a story that proves the existence of God. One day, I was driving behind some boys in a convertible, and we had come to a stop, and they were fooling around. One of them jumped up to stand on the seat, and he was wearing those baggy pants boys wear these days, and are you familiar with the phrase 'Magic Fingers'? That's what happened. He jumped right out of his pants. So don't ever tell me there's no God. There's absolute sufficiency in that event."

I knew what she was talking about. Life is full of things to fill even the loneliest person with glee. You could think of God as The Big Entertainer.

"But remember," Joanne said, "God doesn't play well with others. God is one. He created *us* to work out these group dynamics. God has a learning project going on and we're it. We're concerned with life," she said. "Life is great! Desire is the source of everything good. Do you mind if I eat the other spring roll?"

I didn't.

"I guess I'll have the bat mitzvah," I said. "Can you help me?"

"Certainly," she said. "We will meet once in a while, and, as Isaiah said, we will reason together."

That same month, Beth Evergreen convened an adult b'nai mitzvah class. Seven women would meet for a year and a half, learn Hebrew, split up their Torah portion into seven equal chunks, and become adults sometime in 2005. I went to the first meeting but didn't sign up. Like God himself, apparently, I didn't work well in groups. I thought I could do the whole thing in less than eighteen months. Secretly, I wanted to be a star.

I read a little Isaiah to prepare for my next lunch with Joanne. "He's a nutcase," I reported. "He sounds like he's raving in the desert. Who really wrote all this?"

"Which Isaiah?" Joanne asked.

"What do you mean, *which* Isaiah?"

"Remember, Isaiah is four things at once."

I took out my notebook and pen. For the first time in thirty years, I would take scholarly, as opposed to reporterly, notes.

1. He's George Will. A pundit. He says, "Don't make alliances with Egypt. Stay neutral. Israel is a corridor, and everyone has to pass through the corridor even to get to the bathroom. Watch it."
2. He does poetic prophecy. "It shall come to pass," and that sort of thing.
3. He yells at the people to keep them from drinking too much.
4. He tells the truth to the king. He's the only one who's allowed to do that.

"When I read Isaiah," she concluded, "I have to look up thirty Hebrew words on each page, as opposed to six. And he's very Jerry Seinfeld, full of in-jokes and ironic little jabs."

We were warming up, picking out Bible snippets and talking about them for no particular reason. When I wanted a particular section to study, though, she suggested *Va-Etchanan,* a late summer portion that would come around in six months. Its first words meant "And I pleaded." I could certainly relate to that, but

I didn't pin down the date. If eighteen months was too far away, six was uncomfortably close.

THE 2003 HIGH Holy Days arrived, with four days of four-hour-long services. Even a Catholic wedding lasted only about an hour and a half. Maybe for this reason, Eric became even more moderately religious. He'd attend the evening service for each of the two holy days, and treat the daylight hours like any other.

Coco persisted in being devout.

"What are you going to wear?" she asked, on the eve of Rosh Hashanah. "Could you try to look Jewish?"

Right. A modest dress from Loehmann's, high heels, and a knock-off Gucci handbag. While we're at it, why not shave my head and put on a *sheitel,* the wig Orthodox women wear after marriage? Feh! I'd wear my usual rumpled *shmatte,* but I'd show up. As a potential bat mitzvah, I felt more obligated than ever to examine my soul in the company of my congregation.

Before sundown on Rosh Hashanah, Eric and I went for a mountain-bike ride, stopping for a moment at the top of the most challenging hill, hoping to hear elk bugling, as they do in the fall. We didn't hear anything yet. From the trail, I could see the sanctuary windows of the brand new synagogue, paid for with Jewish money by mountain Jews. During the Yom Kippur fast, as a way of passing time, we could walk slowly over to this meadow and contemplate wildflowers.

That evening the synagogue parking lot was full. Dressed-up people were walking in toward the building from all directions.

The new *shul* shares a driveway with a nursing home. In one window, I saw an old man staring at all the Jews, as absorbed as if he were watching TV.

I knew people enough to say hello. Some were selfless, the kind of people who greeted you even if they'd never met you, brought food, and served on too many committees. You could easily get roped into becoming one of them, I thought. One Saturday morning, I witnessed a woman's conversion ceremony; a week later, she was in charge of the Social Action Committee, collecting tiny hotel shampoos and soaps to give to the homeless. I was impressed by her, but afraid she might suck me in.

The synagogue was once-a-year crowded, but I picked out the familiar cast—the guy who always brings his dog to services; the very old lady whose sons won't take her, so she calls the synagogue secretary for a ride; and the usual handful of ADD boys making their mothers crazy.

As the chatter died down, we began to sing the strange little all-purpose syllables—*diggy diggy lie lie la-li*—intended to put Jews in the mood for prayer. According to tradition, God would be observing us during the next ten days, noting our rights and wrongs in the past year so that he could inscribe us in the Book of Life—if we'd been good—or the Book of Death—if we'd been unusually bad. There was also apparently a Book of In-Between, where most of us end up. This just sounded stupid. I was in a snotty, teenage mood.

"What's so holy about all this guilty hair-tearing?" I wrote, and passed it in a note to Eric.

He thought I misunderstood the purpose of the holiday.

"It's actually about starting with a clean slate," he wrote back. "We don't have a whole holiday dedicated to self-loathing. That's totally un-Jewish."

"Do you argue with God?"

"No, not exactly. I might, maybe, rail. Or say: How is this right?"

We began the *Hashkivenu* prayer, which I never liked. We sang:

Keep us safe throughout the night
till we wake with morning's light
teach us, God, wrong from right.
Amen.

What kind of *farkakteh* God decides I should die while I sleep, but changes his mind if I beg him to spare me? I didn't become a Jew to take up with that kind of micro-manager.

Actually, my frame of reference for God was more automotive than petitionary. I preferred to think of him as a divine engine additive who, if I used him, kept me running smoothly. To throw a rod or slip a timing belt would be only human, and with a little input from God, I would arrange a tune-up and get on down the road.

Maybe that's what people asked God for. Maybe that's what praying was. I wasn't sure because I'd never prayed. Not once.

In *Little Women,* the March girls were always retiring to a closet to cry and pray, emerging as pink and tingly as if they'd had a massage and a *schvitz*. In Vietnam, I saw the serenest monk in the world at prayer in a cave, sitting rocklike through the flash bulbs of German tourists and a cat that kept walking back and forth over his lap. My born-again Christian friends prayed *for* things. They kept people in their prayers. Prayer was said to be cathartic. That sounded good, but a little distant. A lot of things sounded good. Being thin, I'd always liked the sound of that—but just because you wanted it didn't mean you could have it.

For lack of a better plan, I started talking to God because that's what religious people appeared to do. At first, all I could come up with was the kind of thing you'd say at a tennis club: *A little help here! Thank you!* No help materialized.

My biggest freelance job fell through and a half-year's income melted away, and I settled into becoming a mess. With simplistic affirmations swirling in my head—*I am a successful writer with a thick skin and plenty of money*—I got up, ate my own weight in breakfast, got my kids off to school, and often just went back to bed to read books about people who chucked it all and became truck farmers. Or I slept uneasily. Or I took half an Ativan and walked around like a yawning zombie.

Still I talked to God: *I hate you! What good are you?* And that sort of adolescent thing. It diminished about 30 percent of the tension. Not bad, but I hoped for better.

My sister Marina was out of work, too. She got me to meet her at cafes once in a while to brainstorm about our fate.

"Dad says religion is a crutch," I complained, "so where the hell is it when I need it? And I'm always hearing about how faith is for people who can't face reality. So great—I don't *want* to face reality, but I have to."

Marina, who doesn't believe in God, proved to be a better Jew than I was. As she understood it, God was not his own little paramedic crew, but more of a consultant. If you related to him, he could help from a remove, and she had no disdain for people whose psyches operated this way.

"Except when I'm watching football," she said, "and a guy scores a touchdown and he points to the sky or crosses himself real quick, like God rushed over to help. I mean, if that's true, why bother striving to do anything?"

Because she didn't believe, and because she's the type to take the most reasonable step, and because she has not really considered indulging self-pity for more than twenty-four hours, she continued to read Craigslist and do freelance web design work, and then took a course in commercial sewing and began to make custom purses and peddle them to boutiques. I admired her, and sat there, and continued talking to God when I was alone in the car.

Okay, I admit there's nothing crisper than a Colorado sky, and it doesn't escape me that even when it blizzards around here the sun comes out again and melts the snow banks and it's sixty-five degrees in late November. I'll give you that. Although maybe you had nothing to do with it. Still, I know you like it when I appreciate what is.

During this period, just entering the synagogue made me weepy, and not because the services were anything to write home about, just the usual life cycles and holiday progressions: Yom Kippur, Sukkot, Simchat Torah, Shabbat, Shabbat, Shabbat. More because I clung to the idea of following directions.

Coco had started teaching Hebrew school; Gus had just entered the kindergarten religious school class.

"What does a Jew need to know and do?" I asked them.

"A Jew should know Hebrew," Coco said. "They should start learning it *right now.*" She didn't offer to teach me, rightly suspecting that all we'd do was argue.

Gus's answer was lenient. "A Jew should *try* to learn Hebrew. They should do their best."

I went to the bookstore. A book promising to teach me Hebrew in fifteen minutes a day ended up being a primer for modern tourists to Israel. I learned to say "Where is the nearest bathroom?" and "Does anyone speak English?" before seeing that this had nothing to do with Torah. In fact, the Hebrew language inhabited two distinct worlds—an ancient wandering-in-the-desert era and modern times, beginning with the state of Israel in 1948. I could learn specialized words like "vending machine" ("oh-toh-mat") and "Popsicle" ("ar-tik"), but they would never appear in my bat mitzvah.

I switched to *Teach Yourself to Read Hebrew,* which got right into the prayers. "*Ish*" was the word for "man." I got a thrill from "*ish.*" A caveman could have said it five thousand years ago. A nomad.

"'*Ish*' is the fancier word," Joanne observed. "The other one is '*adam,*' which means 'made from dirt.' '*Ish*' is operatic. '*Adam*' is the guy who leaves the toilet seat up."

Hebrew was less complicated than English. For one thing, vowels are only there for beginners. It would be as if, once you were proficient in English, the words "caveman" and "nomad" looked like "CVMN" and "NMD."

Studying Hebrew gave me a noticeable lift. It was better, in its way, than the *New York Times* Sunday crossword—a soothing puzzle to undertake alone. Joanne said that ancient Hebrew actually contains puns, but I knew it would be years before I'd understand them, and even then I might need to have some Aramaic under my belt. It was clear now, where it hadn't been before, that a certain kind of Jew studies this stuff forever and calls it a life well spent.

But I wasn't sure I could be that sedentary. In my early twenties, I'd been a lounger. Now, apparently, I was used to moving around, headed for an antsy middle age. Even my back and aging joints hated to sit still for very long—but that, I feared, was exactly what the most scholarly Jews did. Even as they became Talmudic geniuses, their biceps shriveled.

I was working myself into a philosophical tangle when I happened to hear about Jamie Korngold, the Adventure Rabbi. I saw a picture of her leading a Jewish river trip down the Grand Canyon. She was absolutely buff. Not knowing exactly how her congregation worked, I went ahead and requested an audience with her.

She lived in a Boulder condo with a view of the foothills. She was blond, with the sharply defined quadriceps of a runner and the particular nose tan that comes from spending long hours outside in sunglasses. Her entryway was crowded with skis and snowshoes; her office was lined with scholarly books. She sat across from me at a polished wood library table and waited. *She appears to be a real religious pro*, I thought. *On the other hand, she's at least ten years younger than I am.*

"I wish Judaism involved more sweat," I finally said.

"Me too. Hey, maybe you should come on our women's trip to the Grand Canyon in March. I'm taking a yoga instructor. Think—you could read Torah at the base of the Canyon."

Indoor synagogues didn't seem to interest her much. She talked about the Shabbat evening hikes she led and the Shabbat morning services she held on the slopes at Copper Mountain. Before becoming a rabbi, she'd been an extreme skier, while always remaining a Jew.

"I grew up in a religious household," she said. "It wasn't a choice, it was like breathing. I was thirteen, and I still remember the incredible feeling of accomplishment, of being capable. The rabbi fed me Hebrew words because he was afraid I hadn't learned them, and he was wrong. I still feel like I could have done it without his help. It was very powerful. My dad will still say my older sister's bat mitzvah was the proudest day of his life. So I tried to trump that by becoming a rabbi—I'm kidding, of course."

Growing up in Scarsdale, New York, she attended a large Reform synagogue. She had great affection for her family, but she spent a lot of time traveling away from them, bicycling alone across the country, driving a taxi in Alaska, and singing on the street for tips in Japan. Love of powder skiing led her to settle in Vail, where she worked as a massage therapist to support her habit. Still an enthusiastic Jew, she joined Vail's rudimentary congregation and emerged as one of its most learned members. Because the group had no rabbi of its own, she fell into the habit of leading services and giving advice. The Vail Jews admired her ability to work skiing into sermons. They wanted to hang on to her. Finally, they asked her to consider rabbinic school. She debated between that and becoming a chiropractor, but Judaism won out, and she left Colorado for Hebrew Union College in Cincinnati.

Alone in a world of religion and scholarship, where some people had never heard of a massage therapist, she began running to relieve stress, and she didn't do it in a casual spirit. She entered and finished hundred-mile races, formulating strategy as she ran. She would become something that hadn't yet been invented. Rather than sign on with a congregation, she launched a website: www.adventurerabbi.com.

"Lots of people can have a spiritual experience in a synagogue," she said, "but a lot can't—their spirituality awakens outdoors, maybe reading Torah on top of a mountain. These are people who rebel against the ostentation of bar mitzvahs, who want to go for a hike or rent a bunch of cabins instead."

A lot of those people were under thirty and had drifted from their childhood Judaism. Once they found the Adventure Rabbi, they stuck with her through births, bar mitzvahs, and marriages—one involving a whitewater rafting and camping expedition. She became an outdoor rabbi.

Jewish texts weren't exactly full of sages who had embraced this approach, unless you counted Nachman of Bratslav, a late-eighteenth-century Eastern European rabbi who had led his followers out into the Ukrainian countryside to worship God in the form of nature. I had read some of his poetry and came to think he'd been born three hundred years too early. He could have been a famous hippie rabbi in the 1960s.

The prayer pamphlet Jamie gave out on her Shabbat hikes always quoted Nachman, this passage in particular:

Every blade of grass sings poetry to God
without ulterior motive or alien thoughts—
without consideration or reward.

How good and lovely it is, then,
When one is able to hear this song of the grasses.

I'd never heard this song, I told her, even though I lived surrounded by the woods, my backyard crisscrossed with running
trails, a snowboarding hill only forty-five minutes away. I ran or
walked or biked outdoors almost every day. But I did it in an unquiet
state of mind, wondering how I measured up, why I wasn't faster, or
what daily-life details I might be forgetting during my supposed time
off. There was something weirdly selfish about this train of thought.
I wanted to practice a sweaty, contemplative Judaism instead.

"Your problem is really interesting," Jamie said. "How do you
get your mind to stop? How do you get physical activity to do that?
Used to be, I just ran for a long time. The first hour and a half was
for cleansing my brain, and the rest was actually useful. But then
my life kicked in. I don't have time for six-hour runs anymore."

She walked over to the bookshelf and began scanning titles.
"You need to think about creating a kind of sacred time. Abraham
Joshua Heschel says that in Judaism we don't have sacred space as
much as sacred time. We can't just walk into a building and feel
religion. You can't just go out onto a trail and find God. Shabbat
is only Friday night unless in our intention we *make* it Shabbat. If
I were you, I'd concentrate on that."

On *time?* Time wasn't sweaty, and Shabbat didn't conjure up im-
ages of motion. I'd been hoping she'd tell me to do something with
my body I'd never done before—like those Buddhist monks who
run all night, every night, and do it in the presence of God. I'd
never run a marathon before. Maybe if I believed enough, I could?

"Think about this," she said. "Shabbat is our most important holiday and it comes every week. Why?" she asked, dragging me back to time.

Well, I thought. *If I must.*

Shabbat was important because God took a weekly rest—it was right there in the first chapter of the Torah. Orthodox Jews appeared to be passionately in love with Shabbat. They called it "sweet," and reluctantly said goodbye to it on Saturday at sundown. During those sweet twenty-four hours, "work" was off limits—no switching on electric lights, no business dealing, no cooking, no phone calls, no car rides, no breaking a sweat. Nothing but rest. The very thought of it made me want to jump out of my skin.

"Play with it anyway," Jamie suggested. "Try to find one way that fits and is realistic and relevant. If you go snowboarding, make it Shabbat snowboarding. When you're on the chairlift, talk to your family about text. You might love being out of touch for the day. I do. I love the candles and the wine cup, and I really do feel sad when it's over."

I thought it was a strange way to hear the songs of the grasses, but said I'd give it a try.

Shabbat: That's a thing a Jew needs to know and do. I'd do it, definitely, right after Sukkot. Eric and Coco built our family's first *sukkah* out of old two-by-fours and fallen aspen limbs. We hung seed packets and gourds from the roof, as close as we could come to approximating an Israeli harvest, and invited a big group of *goyim* over to eat with us.

An early snow came and covered the *sukkah* with a white canopy, which was so beautiful we decided never to take it down. Was that allowed?

"Ma," Coco said, "if you really want to know the rules, you ask the Orthodox."

THE AD FOR Aharon's Mile Chai Judaica read: "Books! Music! Sacred texts! Everything for the Jewish Home!" Coco and I went down to Denver on the quiet Sunday of Thanksgiving weekend, when entire neighborhoods seemed comatose from too much food. Aharon's was just reopening after the twenty-four-hour Sabbath. It was located on the ground floor of a strip mall, small and fluorescent lit.

Inside, klezmer music blasted from a boom box. On display were various things I'd never seen up close: bar mitzvah greeting cards, yarmulkes, Jewish snow globes—everything but a Moses action figure.

Coco, who had decided to keep kosher in our House of *Trayf*, gravitated to the specialized pot labels, knives, and soap scrubbies, all coded for meat or milk. Before long, she was talking to Chava Weiss, Aharon's wife, who answered her questions evenly, without any of the missionary excitement I'd seen among Christians when they met someone who might want to sign up.

"You can get an online pen pal to learn Torah with," Chava told Coco. "It's completely free of charge." She wore a long skirt and black head scarf.

Two cute boys in their early twenties came in. They looked like any other outdoorsy Colorado youth, like guys you'd see on the Pearl Street Mall in Boulder, in jeans and Polartec vests—and yarmulkes. They went to the back room to look at Talmuds and tefillin, the little leather boxes containing bits of scripture that Orthodox men strap to their right arms and foreheads during prayer.

"This is Orthodox?" I asked.

"Well, I'm *modern* Orthodox," Chava said, "but I don't care for labels. I do follow the rules of modesty. No low-cut necklines. All my dresses below the knees. I don't generally wear pants, and one of the things I'm working on, because God knows I always need to work on something, is covering my hair. Wearing a *sheitel* is uncomfortable. I had one, but I barbecued it standing over the grill. I try always to wear a hat to *shul*."

"Could you go out for a run?" I asked.

"I could exercise at home," she said, as if the thought had never occurred to her, "but going outside in shorts? No."

I was sincerely intrigued by anyone who could live without sweat, or a pair of sweat pants, for that matter.

"I let my daughters wear denim skirts," she offered.

"Can they be friends with someone who's not Jewish?" Coco asked.

"Oh, sure. I'd have to make sure there was a kosher kitchen, though. If not, I'd have to pack them food and paper plates. But I've been doing that for years. When they go to a birthday party, they bring their own forks and spoons and their own piece of cake."

"Have you always lived this way?"

"No," Chava said. "I am a Jew by choice."

Chava and Aharon had moved to Denver from suburban Boise. They'd both been raised without much religion at all. After they married, they attended a big Methodist church, where Sunday services were broadcast on live TV.

"We got tired of being *entertained* in church," Chava said primly. "We were looking for something closer to God's word. In doing the research, we came to the conclusion that Judaism made the most sense." Almost overnight, Chava and Aharon became not just Jews, but fervent Jews. I was impressed—grasping the most elementary basics had taken me five years.

"Hey, where are those tefillin cases?" Aharon yelled from a back room.

"Right in front of your face," Chava said calmly. Aharon came out and began foraging through a cabinet. He was short and round, with a yarmulke stuck to his balding head, looking exactly like my stereotype of an Orthodox Jew, as if he'd been that way since birth. "Idaho native" and "former Methodist" were not descriptions that would have occurred to me. The tefillin cases he finally found were made of purple ripstop nylon and looked like something you'd take on a backpacking trip. "They're neat, aren't they?" Chava said. "Developed in the Israeli army."

"How on earth did you learn enough Judaism to stock this store?" I asked.

"We asked the rabbis," she said. "We learned the rules. You read books, you talk to rabbis."

I must have looked dubious. Whatever I did want to learn, it wasn't what head-covering to wear, how to package kosher snacks for my kids to take into the menacing outside world, or how to take the words of the Torah literally, when I was already quite clear that big chunks of it were either delusions or metaphors. Surely I had different issues to discuss with rabbis, if I ever got the chance.

"Don't you see?" Chava said, as if she felt a little sorry for me. "Real Judaism spells out how to be a Jew. We follow the commandments, and there's freedom there. You will do this at this time, that at that time. You *know* where all the boundaries are, the fences, the structure. It's very comforting."

It seemed unlikely I would ever make peace with structure, let alone find it comforting. When I was nineteen, I had lasted only an hour as a telephone solicitor, not because it's an appalling job, but because they wanted me to read from a script printed on a laminated sheet, the same way every time. "Hello, ma'am. Would you like to save seventy percent on most household items? Doesn't that sound good, ma'am?" I ended up at this lame job as a direct result of dropping out of college, which had also seemed too structured.

People like me were known to suddenly adopt rigid religion— shave their heads, eat only bowls of rice, rise at four in the morning to chant. But I had as much chance of grafting that kind of program onto myself as of suddenly becoming a professional tap dancer.

Coco used her own allowance to buy a package of MILK and MEAT labels.

I went home and defiantly ate a BLT. I tried, but I didn't understand these people.

Three days later, I had coffee with another Orthodox woman.

"You don't understand us," said Lori Palatnik. "A lot of people don't. People think we're religious so we don't have to think for ourselves. Ha! Not thinking is letting a bunch of gay men in Italy tell you how short your skirt should be."

Her own skirt was an elegant, calf-length denim number. She was very attractive, as my dad would say, and didn't appear to come from an insular, restricted world. Her hair was short, dark, and shiny; a hands-free cell phone was connected to her ear by an unobtrusive cord. She apologized for that, but she had so many speaking engagements in the works, and she didn't want to miss any. *And* she had five kids, to whom she acted as the perfect Jewish mother. *And* she had a happy marriage to a vivacious-sounding rabbi. She made me feel like an utter *schlep*.

We met at Starbucks, which is kosher, she said, as long as you don't eat the baked goods. Like Chava, Lori was an Orthodox Jew by choice.

"I was raised just a typical North American Jew," she told me. "We went to the temple three times a year—the thirteen and out club. I had a good job in advertising. I even won an award for writing a Christmas ad. Jews are great at Christmas—just look at Irving Berlin."

She'd never dated a Jewish man, and was astonished when one of her sisters suddenly turned Orthodox. *At least she's not handing out flowers at the airport,* she thought. But while backpacking in Europe, a schedule change forced her plane to land in Israel, and that opened up an unthinkable possibility.

"Maybe God grabbed my sleeve and said, 'Hey you, we need to talk,'" she said, "because you just can't imagine what it's like in Israel. On Fridays, even the most secular Jew is wishing you a *Shabbat shalom*. On Purim, the bus driver is wearing a clown suit."

She tried to return to her old life in Ottawa but almost immediately was offered a chance to go back to Israel on a fellowship.

"My gentile boss was actually proud of me," she remembered. "If he'd been Jewish, never. Jews are much more suspicious of Jewish things." The fellowship ended, but she stayed in Jerusalem, teaching aerobics to housewives in their living rooms because, after all, it wouldn't be modest to go to an outside gym. Religion crept into her days. Living where she did, it wasn't hard to learn the basic mitzvahs, and it got easier when she started dating the rabbi she later married.

Judaism just isn't that complicated, she said. She and her husband, Yaacov, have made a joint career of explaining it, of getting people jazzed about Orthodoxy. Just follow three basic rules to be Jewish: keep kosher, celebrate a strict Shabbat, and observe the "laws of family purity," which specify when during a woman's reproductive cycle she can have sex with her husband, and how and when she must purify herself in the ritual bath.

"But that's it!" she said. "The Torah says not to be a robot. These laws are meant to open you up."

I didn't do any of these things, but rather than hold it against me, Lori invited me to spend twenty-four hours at her house, really experiencing Shabbat. It sounded like something I ought to do. But again I had an uncomfortable vision of that world, with its women in long dresses cooking and cleaning, stiflingly mature.

"You don't seem to grasp that I have a very rewarding life," she said. "My husband and I have *the* secret to being in an excellent marriage and staying committed. How many couples can say that?"

The secret, again, was family purity. Two weeks on, two weeks off. I couldn't flat out say it *wouldn't* invigorate a marriage. But delayed gratification was another thing I hadn't had much success with, so far. So, she said, make the effort.

"It used to be, you could just be Jewish by birth and it would mean something," she told me. "These days, though, you're either in or out, and if you're not keeping kosher, you're just not very Jewish. Nowadays there's so much intermarriage, only the real Jews will survive. The others will fade away because they have no values. Lucy and Ricky used to sleep in single beds. Now Ricky sleeps with Fred in one big bed."

"You can't be a gay Jew?" I asked incredulously.

"Oh, you can, but you're making a mistake. Eating *trayf* is also a mistake. You can make a mistake and be as Jewish as my husband the rabbi. Only God can judge. But you're definitely making a mistake."

According to Lori, understanding the basic rules was *simple*. But I *simply* would not go along with religious zealots who opposed homosexuality on principle. They could pick out bits of the Torah to justify their positions. *But,* I thought, *they could also bite me!* Jews are supposed to be inclusive—to invite the stranger in their midst over for dinner. *As for gay Jews,* I thought, *love is love and it pleases God. Clearly. Absolutely.*

It was fun to have a strong opinion.

Next, of course, I went looking for a gay Jew, and ended up with Bobbi Furer. She was seventy-three and not feeling well. An infection had developed where the doctor had made an incision two weeks ago for a degenerative bladder condition.

"My faith is being tested," she announced, as she led me into her kitchen. "My primitive belief in a God that's going to help me isn't worth beans. The childlike longing for the old man in the sky. Blah blah blah."

"Why won't God help you?" I asked.

"It's still a mystery. Our cantor told me to say the *Shema* like a mantra, when I go to bed and when I wake up. I said it. Nothing changed."

Until she got up to answer the door, Bobbi had been lying in bed making her own cremation plans and feeling infuriated by, as opposed to afraid of, death. She kept thinking about Christian Scientists. Although she'd been a Jew most of her life, she felt free to experiment with any belief that seemed to have potential. *Whatever's wrong with me is all in my head,* she thought, trying it out.

"My partner, Linda, thinks I'm crazy. I believe in reincarnation, too," she said, as if daring me to argue. "Look at the trees. They're dormant right now, but they'll be back. Maybe I will, too, after I die. Baptists—their faith is really strong. They don't care so much about dying because they really believe they're going to a beautiful heaven. Maybe I should have been a Baptist."

I felt for her, trying to make sense of what might be her final illness, while looking back on all the directions her life had taken. She'd been a traditionally Orthodox woman for the first half of her life, but after a long career as a therapist, had finally realized the hypocrisy of it, and had come out at forty-five. "It took me years to get up the guts to do it," she said, "but the times were terrible back then—you were queer, sick, a fairy. In those days I had a rabbi I talked to a lot, kind of a family therapist. Even he said: 'I love you, but I can't accept you.'" Now she was deep into the second half of her life as a gay Jew who no longer kept two sets of dishes or went to the *mikvah*.

Bobbi wouldn't let me help make the tea, but sat me down at her kitchen table and waited on me. She was little, maybe five foot two, and thin. She folded her small hands on the table and looked at me expectantly, from the middle of her Jewish kitchen. There was a mezuzah on the front door, a seder plate on the kitchen wall, and a family photo album on the coffee table, full of pictures of relatives who'd died in the Holocaust.

"Oh honey, how sweet," she said, when Linda came home from work with a bouquet of flowers for Shabbat, still wearing her Home Depot employee's badge. "She's fourteen years younger than me," Bobbi informed me, "and a nice Jewish girl, too. She converted."

"We were at an Orthodox funeral, black hats and everything," Linda recalled for me, "and I thought: *Hot day out, I could convert to Judaism, boy, I could go for an iced latte.* It was just one of those moments."

The two women were now members of one of Denver's biggest Reform synagogues. "Hate the rabbi, love the cantor," Linda said. "It works, for now."

Bobbi had lived in the same house more than forty years, ever since she married her second husband, Max, in 1960. It sits in a very Jewish suburb; the neighbors on each side are Orthodox, one of them a concentration camp survivor.

"I don't know if you could call this a Jewish home," Linda said, "but we took the *trayf* out of the kitchen, at least. We take what we want from the religion."

"I believe what Einstein did," Bobbi said. "God is the earth. I've been able to think that without help from a rabbi, and I'm still a Jew. I wish I could tell you what my rules are, but I can't. I'm just a Jew."

"Me too," I said, leaving Bobbi's house with my mood considerably lightened.

Okay. I was just a Jew.

I did not:

Keep kosher
Play mahjong
Observe the Sabbath
Bargain
Folk dance
Have any new info about the existence of God

I did:

Make a decent challah
Say the blessing over it with my family before dinner
Go to *shul* once in a while
Talk to God
Raise Jewish kids
Cohabit with a Jewish man
Honor my father. Or try.

He wanted to go out and he didn't care where, as long as he could drive the magic new Suburban, which had turned out to be magic indeed. Dad had signed himself up for a voluntary driving exam for seniors. Whoever passed him—with an excellent score—was just plain crazy. Dad drove, all right, hunched over the wheel, blasting classical music and never turning his arthritic neck to the right or left. I should have insisted on grabbing his keys, but I didn't. *His days are numbered,* I'd think, as he glided obliviously through a red light.

It was a time of hot turkey sandwiches—"with real turkey, not that loaf crap they inject with water"—and I got used to holding open a restaurant door with one hand, untangling his oxygen tube with the other, and wondering how the entrance to a ground floor restaurant could have so many stairs leading nowhere. Once inside, Dad would pitch himself after the hostess on his numb feet, occasionally clutching the back of some surprised diner's chair. It was hair raising, but he always got to the table.

He spent much of each lunch date reminding me that he existed, had a past, had done remarkable things. When he said, "What's new with you?" he really meant, "What have you done or thought that leads directly back to me?"

We ate matzo ball soup and chopped liver and herring—none as good as what he made at home—and he'd tell me about driving around Manhattan in the fifties, listening to his police scanner and showing up at crime scenes before all the other reporters. I had come to see that some of these stories were only partly true, but it didn't really bother me. I knew him for a schmoozer, and it must have been fun to eavesdrop on those police calls. He had always found his way into other people's conversations.

He did this on elevators, with strangers. He turned small talk into big talk. He'd discuss the weather, but only if a hurricane was coming. During long car rides, he used to pretend to be various taciturn people: a Maine lobsterman, a congressman with something to hide, the lock tender who moved the boats from Peconic Bay into Long Island Sound. My job was to talk to these imaginary people until they opened up. To this day, I don't like quiet elevators.

My father didn't do these things so much anymore. His life was narrow.

"What are we all going to do for Christmas this year?" he asked me. "All right, all right, I forgot. What about that *farkakteh* Chanukah then?" If we didn't gather in one room for many hours, there would be a terrible shortage of gossip in the coming year, no reason to buy a spiral ham, and no upheaval, which you had to have.

"Should I make *gehachte*?" he asked, using the Yiddish word for chopped liver. "It's important to a Jew." The perfect chopped liver recipe was handed down to him long ago by Sascha Jacobson, a musician and good friend of Chotzie's family. "We all really loved food, but Sascha just about lived for it," he remembered. "My father would get hysterical about Sascha's need for radishes and sour cream, with the little green scallions and of course, *gehachte*. Sascha taught me to make it with the onions really, really brown, not pale, like some people do it. It takes a while, but it's the best."

A few days later, I squeezed into my father's narrow kitchen and watched him chop onions and sway at the giant restaurant stove that barely fit between the back door and the counter. He wheeled around as he talked, holding a hot skillet, on a temporary mission.

AT CONGREGATION BETH Evergreen, there was gossip—just in time for the 2004 High Holy Days. Rabbi Baskin had resigned! The official explanation was that the congregation had grown enough to need a full-time rabbi, and Rabbi Baskin wasn't interested in the job. But he'd also moved down to the flatlands, which struck some members as a little snooty. (He'd never liked us to call him by his first name, either.) He was no longer technically a mountain Jew. So a rabbi search committee was formed, and it was working overtime. Joanne Greenberg was part of it.

"I really fell in love with this one guy," she confided. "I was all ready for the wedding—had my shoes dyed to match my dress, and everything. But then he had some kind of personal crisis and now we have to start all over again."

Meanwhile, the board hired Rabbi Rami Shapiro to take us through Rosh Hashanah and Yom Kippur. Rami Shapiro had had his own congregation in Miami for nearly twenty years but had recently moved to Tennessee to set up shop as a "stand-up mystic" who traveled to spiritual centers—yoga retreats, Catholic monasteries—to share his particular brand of Judaism. He was a freelance rabbi, and compared to Rabbi Baskin, a total hippie. He had grown up Orthodox, then come under the influence of Rabbi Zalman Shachter-Shalomi, the eighty-year-old father of the Jewish Renewal movement. Reb Zalman lives in Boulder, where it's not unusual for a Jew to meditate using Tibetan prayer beads.

The last thing I expected was to develop a spiritual crush on a guy I didn't know, to whom I was never introduced, and who, even though I took to sitting practically at his feet, didn't pay any attention to me. But half an hour into the evening Rosh Hashanah service, I felt like George Harrison meeting the Maharishi. It was raining. We could see lightning through the ceiling windows. When a thunderclap interrupted Rabbi Rami's sermon, he whipped out his cell phone.

"Yes?" he said. "Oh. I see." Then he turned toward us and said: "It's *Gawd!*" (He learned the rural Baptist pronunciation from listening to Christian radio stations in Tennessee.)

He told us that "Rosh Hashanah" literally meant "Head of the Year," and invited us to translate that as "change your head," to move from what he called "narrow mind" to "spacious mind." Explaining this, he walked and stretched, laughed and riffed:

"God doesn't change—God *is* change. You and I are God, we're little Gods running around. And yet we live as if we were separated from God. The Torah tells you right here that we're supposed to till the soil, and the soil we're supposed to till is up to us. But our soil gets hard-packed and lifeless. God tells Abraham, basically, to do three things: One: *Lech lecha,* which means to get *out* of your country, your king, your culture. Two: Get out of your *father's* house. Every place in the world is holy ground if you can take your shoes off and free yourself. Three: *Change your head!* Ask yourself: Can I live for ten days drama-free?"

No drama? How could that be Jewish? Well, I might give it a shot if it meant I could become funny and wise and entertaining, like my hero, Rami Shapiro. The usual four-hour High Holy Day services were passing like forty-five-minute Seinfeld routines, and drama-free began to sound okay.

"Religion isn't holy," he said, "it's just a story, because God is bigger than anything, even religions, so we tell each other stories to make sense of it. I would never say that one story is better—or truer—than another, and the only ones I distrust are the ones who claim their story is best. That anyone who doesn't believe it should be killed. As for me, it just turned out that Judaism was the story that resonated. So I'm a Jew." A Jew who believed in solitary meditation and long, unvarnished conversations with God.

"I do it during my morning walk, because I might as well get some aerobic benefit. I just say, 'Hello, Mother,' which is what I like to call God—I know, I know, paging Dr. Freud—and I thank her for all my blessings, and then I tell her what I need today, and then I walk about five miles, fast."

On the morning before *Kol Nidre*, he left his Colorado hotel room just off the interstate and started his daily walk/talk. Burger King was in his way, so he walked right through it. On the way, he picked up a paper placemat printed with the words "You CAN have it your way!"

"Well, can you?" he asked us later. "Nope. You can't."

You could have it the *spacious* way, though. You could change your head. In spite of my lifelong abhorrence of contemplative practice, I went to a Rabbi Rami meditation workshop, where I hoped to be a star student and attract his notice—until he asked us please not to come up to him and tell him how well our meditations had worked, how in the zone we were, because there was no good or bad way to meditate. It wasn't an accomplishment. You didn't get a prize. It was a practice; you practiced it.

So I lay on my back breathing and reciting the *Shema*. I walked around the room, inwardly repeating the words all the heavy hitters in the Torah said when God spoke to them. *Hineini! Here I am!* I learned a kabbalist chant taught to Rami by some Senegalese Sufi who had learned it from Reb Zalman Shachter-Shalomi. Rami had a million words and phrases to describe God. My favorite was "that which is happening now."

MY HOUSE WAS built directly on top of a granite outcrop on the side of a south-facing mountain. In autumn, which lasts about three weeks, the aspens turn briefly gold while the pines stay inscrutably green. This time of year the moon looks like a giant, celestial hub cap. Outside, under the moon, you might see a bear cruising for a suet bird-feeder or a mountain lion waiting to kill a deer. Then it starts to snow. I didn't necessarily love this landscape—I always felt more at home near an ocean, or on a flat expanse of prairie. But since I was living on the side of a mountain, I decided to pay attention.

I found myself staring at birds, though I was no birdwatcher. Migrating geese—how did they know the pattern, and where to go, and what did it sound like up there, in formation? I sat outside among the hummingbirds, who were whooping it up in their last few days before heading back to Mexico, swaggering, always fighting each other for a taste of something sweet. They were such little birds. It seemed to imply that although God was very big, God was also involved in miniature things, for a reason that might even involve me. Maybe, with assistance from the right bird, I could connect. Maybe the bird had been put there, in all his mariachi glory, to take me out of my head.

At dusk and dawn, I heard bull elks bugling with pent-up lust, their cows chirping. I found their sharp, bitter smell in places where the grass was matted down. God had given them a way to express what they wanted, not from the universe or anything, just from the nearest female elk.

Gus pointed out that the shofar and bugling of elk are essentially the same thing, at the same time of year. I finally decided to set a date for my bat mitzvah.

"So, I'd like *Va-Etchanan*," I said breezily to Neshama, the Beth Evergreen administrator.

"Already taken."

"By who?"

"Some thirteen-year-old kid. Who do you think?"

I ended up with *Ki Tavo* ("When you come into the land.") It would fall on September 24, 2005, and I would have about ten months to get ready.

"Who the hell am I to do this?" I wrote to Joanne. I wrote her via snail mail because I liked getting real letters back. They were crafted on an old manual typewriter by Joanne's part-time secretary. "Will all the teenagers think I'm trying to take a piece of them? I haven't even talked to the Ritual Committee yet."

"I am *on* the Ritual Committee, you ninny," she answered. "So talk to *me*. And in answer to your question: Who the hell are you? Who cares? And good luck."

Good luck, she meant, with the following tasks:

Learning to sing my Torah and *haftarah* in Hebrew
Studying the texts until they became my story, as Rabbi Rami
would say. Giving a speech to explain it.

We also thought maybe I should sew a dress.

"A storyteller always makes her own clothes," Joanne said. "It's part of separating this world from that."

I intended to pay close attention to anything that was concrete about a bat mitzvah. I'd be involved in a kind of construction project—building my language and singing skills, studying Torah, making a dress.

At the fabric store, I bought a pattern for a reproduction 1930s afternoon gown full of impossible curves, especially when I'd sewn nothing but the straight lines of quilts. The saleswoman told me not to buy silk, as it would make me "sweat like a hog." I asked her to cut me yards of white rayon covered with blue and yellow flowers. In the polyester thread and invisible zipper section, I ran into Burke, a guy from my husband's volunteer fire department. He was blond and buff, wearing a department T-shirt.

"You better stop trying to pull over that bias tape display," he told his eight-year-old daughter.

"*Abba*," she said, "can you make me a Torah cover?"

Burke was *Jewish*?

No, he said. Messianic—a Jew for Jesus, who keeps kosher, reads Hebrew, and doesn't drive on the Sabbath. If Jesus did all that, he explained, why shouldn't he?

The Messianics in town—there are more every day—are friendlier than we are. When I met a family that had been to a

Passover seder, it was usually a Messianic celebration. My gut impulse was to keep my distance—who were they to call themselves Jews? Instead, Burke and I talked sewing. He started back in his Boy Scout days, sewing to earn a merit badge, and then began making hunting clothes as well as girls' dresses with smocking and pleats. Just like Joanne, he was a lifetime seamstress. A man who matches this description is so rare there doesn't seem to be a word for him. A seamster? Was there a seamster's union? Of course there was. A hundred years ago, the Lower East Side was full of male tailors walking to work with their sewing machines on their shoulders.

I took my raw materials to Joanne's. Albert was walking around in the background with a transistor radio plugged into his ear. We folded the fabric several different ways, yanking it until it began to behave.

"I'll show you how to cut and mark and sew, too," she said. "I know this stuff. I come from a long line of pattern makers, and my family used to have a chain of stores in New York. Subway Silks, it was called. I used to work there, but then they told me if I wanted to help the family business, I'd do them a favor and quit."

She got out her supplies—the purple tracing paper, the glass-headed pins, the hand-sharpened scissors—and began to show me what to do. In cutting fabric with her, I was sewing together a tradition for myself, learning to use what women (and Burke) had always used. The weather cooperated—soon, the first snowstorm of the season brought a curtain down around us. Joanne talked to herself using sentence fragments and a private language. "Pass me that *remlick* over there," she'd say, and I'd know what she was talking about. There was no need to talk a lot. It was parallel play, the stuff they attribute to two-year-olds. I had spent many, many hours with my two daughters this way.

I TRIED TO see my father once a week, but felt not quite guilty enough when two weeks slipped by. Then I would come down the mountain and take him out, while Marina and Ryan enjoyed the illusion that they were leading a normal life as a young married couple renovating an old house. Meanwhile, Dad continued to live on in spite of his body. Every week had its various medical appointments, where he would socialize with nurses and experience some kind of pain. At first, Marina, Jenny, and I thought we could keep track of his conditions, but even the doctors had trouble doing that, what with all the competing meds swirling in his system. There was no prognosis. We talked about preparing ourselves for his death, but never managed to get weepy and miss him in advance, because whenever we tried, he'd come into the room and do something annoying, such as leaving his teeth on the kitchen counter, or something endearing, such as writing five letters to Coco in one night, each with a separate envelope and stamp. And once in a rare while, something fatherly. He believed in electronic solutions to emotional problems, and when I was having trouble finding work he took me out and bought me an expensive sound system, the idea being that very loud music could cure depression. Preferably Wagner, and he gave me a CD of greatest hits just to be sure.

His theory held. When I stood in my living room with Valkyrie music raging around me, I felt very good. The dogs skulked outside. I experimented with the volume knob. It was intoxicating. My daughters came in from the trampoline wondering what the hell was going on, but I didn't hear their yells for the longest time.

Dad spent most of his time reading, sleeping, and writing long letters to his email list. Once in a while he hobbled down the stairs to cook up some fatty passions—three or four eggs, sunny-side-up, in butter. Or, just to keep his diabetes cooking along, a glass half full of seltzer, half of sticky red grenadine syrup.

Three times each week, he staggered out to the garage, got into his giant car, and drove himself to dialysis, where he knew everybody and listened to Uncle Jascha on his iPod. Unable to lose interest in the possibility of romance, he asked a thirty-year-old dialysis nurse out to dinner. They had a pleasant evening at a sushi bar. She told him all her troubles, and there were plenty.

The nurse wasn't the only woman in his life. He had quarreled with his official girlfriend, Jane, a retired journalist, because he hadn't told her when his 1956 girlfriend, Gloria Steinem, came to town and spent a quiet evening with him. It had only been one friendly, platonic night, despite what the local gossip column said. (And guess who gave them the item?) After a while, Jane forgave my father, and she was part of his feeble whirl again. You're never too old for a whirl, was his opinion.

"People don't understand that," he told Coco, who was fourteen. "People say if you're young, you can't fall in love. But if you think you're in love, you are. It's not up to other people to judge. What do they know?"

In January 2005 I brought Coco along to a Dad dinner even though it was a school night, because I needed her to take up some conversational slack. He seemed to want to tell her about life, and she seemed to want to listen. That was great—I could sit with a glass of wine and stare into the middle distance. Sometimes the strain of being a Jew around my father wore me out. "What are you up to these days?" he'd ask—but I wasn't about to mention learning Hebrew or reading Leviticus. So I'd have to dig around for rude gossip.

I'd been fighting with Coco about Israel. She wanted to go there on a teen excursion; I didn't want her to get blown up by a car bomb.

"So let her go," Dad said. "You can't spend your whole life avoiding risks."

Coco smiled triumphantly. Yeah, yeah—they were right.

After that, I excused myself from the rest of the conversation. Close relatives require such constant nurturing, and I was really so lousy at it. I fell into my regular habit of guessing what people were thinking. What was the deal with the aged waitress with the big hair and turquoise nails? *You have to doll up if you're looking for tips,* I imagined her explaining. I didn't hear a word of the conversation between my father and my older daughter.

"He was asking about school," Coco told me as we drove home. "I told him my grades weren't that good. He said he never got good grades himself. He was kind of on my side, I thought. But then he said he knew I could use that excuse, but I shouldn't. He said it was the kind of excuse *he* used to use, but that I was too good for it. I'm too smart and pretty," she said, rather happily.

I had never discussed grades with Dad. School, he always told me, was an annoyance that got in the way of life. And all he ever told me about love was that it would break my heart, which it did for the first few decades. And yet, he said, if you didn't have someone to lean on, you would fall apart. This had been true for most of his life, but it no longer was. At seventy-eight, he had suddenly decided *not* to fall apart. The minute he got carted off to the hospital, he'd start to fight. Because his veins had almost completely collapsed, no one could ever get an IV started but they'd spend forty-five minutes trying to stick him anyway. He usually ended up with a tube going right into the artery in his neck—triumphant because the nurses hadn't killed him, and neither had pain.

In late January, he was back in the hospital, bristling with tubes and monitors, holding court in a hospital nightie while waiting impatiently for a foot operation. He was cranky, yet popular. As usual, his roommate, who lived on the other side of the flimsy curtain divider, was a zombie who did nothing but watch sports on TV or slip in and out of a coma. Certainly, he had nothing to say to his relatives, and Dad was happy to take up the slack, especially when the visitors were female. I got used to being clutched at in hallways by teary women who told me they wouldn't know what to do or where to turn if they couldn't talk to my father. Nurses usually spent lots of time in his room, too—he was high maintenance, but he also made them laugh. Some of the nurses were male, which surprised and irritated my father. What were they, a bunch of *fegelehs*? But they usually ended up having something in common—pheasant hunting, motorcycles, or golden retrievers. Soon, he'd be arranging presents for the staff—Marina's custom purses, mail-order steaks, and symphony tickets.

I stayed with him until the codeine put him to sleep. Later, Marina and Ryan came by with Chinese, but he was too sleepy to eat it, so they left. A few hours later, he stopped breathing altogether. In the absence of a Do Not Resuscitate order, medics rushed in and broke four of his ribs while performing CPR until he was alive again, if unconscious. No one knew what had happened. He might have had a heart attack or a stroke.

"Your father is quite desperately ill," the doctor said. "You should come right away."

When Marina and I got there, Dad was so restless they'd had to tie his hands to the bed so he wouldn't pull out his breathing tube. The nurses kept coming in to put meds in his IV. Then the dialysis cart arrived, and his blood was changed as he lay unconscious. Gruesome, I thought, but I knew he wouldn't agree. If you had to get new blood three times a week to stay alive, fine. Marina and I had the strange sensation of bursting with health.

At home, I walked outside and said *"Hineini"* and watched myself thinking, *Ah, here I am practicing New Age Judaism in the beautiful outdoors. How serene.* I didn't feel serene at all. I felt like getting a bigger bang for my buck where God was concerned, but talking to God had become a reflex so I kept doing it.

"Hello, Mother," I said in front of a suburban car dealership in winter, the air full of the smell of stock yard, incipient snow, and low-trapped exhaust. "I need you to unclog my brain, and fast.

Other people channel their worries into creating significant works of art and battling deadly diseases. By contrast, I can barely stand the tension of having to pick up a hundred boxes of Girl Scout cookies and separate them into piles, and my father is unconscious, but not dead. And the car I brought in for an oil change needs four hundred dollars of extra work. My father got himself a magic car, and what do I have? A minivan. So thank you for everything, Ma, but this is an ugly place, and I've been exposed to some ugly shit. Am I supposed to enjoy being shooed out of the room so the nurse can mop up my father's "fluids"? Remind me that I love life. Thank you. E. B. White says never to use this phrase, but Thank You in Advance."

Then I felt closer to humanity—if not to religious people, then to people who walk down sidewalks talking to themselves. It became a little easier to go to my father's hospital room and just sit there, because that's all there was to do. That, and look forward to a period of rest.

WEEKLY REST WAS an actual commandment. If we didn't need it, why would life's tension crank up so hard, every single week? The time was absolutely right for trying out the concept of Shabbat. The Adventure Rabbi had suggested I start with some kind of observance, if only on a chairlift. I emailed Rabbi Rami for his opinion.

"As far as where to start," he wrote, "I don't think there is a one-size-fits-all answer. It depends on the person. Since I associate religion with story, I would suggest that one become familiar with the stories."

The sun was to set at 4:59 P.M.—as an adult bat mitzvah, I decided to concern myself with such things. After lunch on Friday, I settled in with the *Code of Jewish Law* and tried to pick out the most elementary guidelines: Don't drive, carry money, or answer the phone. Light candles. Bless your kids, and have a nice meal. Study Torah. Don't work.

The *Code,* written in 1924, was full of minutia about saddles, halters, and bridles, but never mentioned the internal combustion engine. It had nothing to do with me, which made it as fascinating as eavesdropping. Who were these readers who required such infinitesimal particulars as to what might constitute working on the Sabbath?

Could you, for instance, wring out a dish towel on Shabbat? Yes, unless the towel is white. It's harder to keep white things clean, but colored things don't show the dirt as much, therefore you can wring them out because it doesn't *remind* you of work. You can't kill bugs other than lice, because lice make it hard to take pleasure in Shabbat, which you're *not* allowed *not* to do. You're not supposed to carry things on Shabbat, so refrain from "carrying" between your legs those bits of rag with which you soak up your menstrual flow. Unless you'd be embarrassed not to—embarrassment on Shabbat is bad.

Was there any connection between this and modern Judaism? Did the eighteenth-century Chasids struggle with and mold these rules for themselves, or were they blindly obedient?

Clean, clean, clean! Cook, cook, cook! Dress in "fine garments"! Clip your finger- and toenails. Bake *three* challahs. Think of God as an intimidating weekend guest, and remember to cover the bread with a cloth while you bless the wine. "That's so the bread won't be embarrassed," said Gus, who had just learned this in Hebrew school.

Friday night is for three-quarter-time music, a fish dinner, and sex. Saturday afternoon is for four-four melodies, meat, and naps—in other words, sex. Saturday night, *havdalah,* requires a light dairy meal and the singing of slow songs. And sex, probably.

Don't let the *goyim* work for you on Shabbat—unless you need them to light the stove for heat, or flick on a light switch, neither of which are kosher. No boiling gravy, either, or grinding homemade mustard in a mortar. Where did that leave a person who found it relaxing to knead bread? Or my friend Jane, a busy attorney whose favorite zone-out is to stir risotto for a half hour, which is, she says, exactly long enough to drink one beer?

Shabbat is a day of rest. Which meant I could forget about my father and whether I needed a rest from him, and whether such thoughts were proper or abominable, and how you continually honor a guy who never stops being needy. I don't remember who translated that for me as "quit rushing and schlepping for a day," but it sounded great. Still, though, why was it so important to set the table with finery, creating a lot of extra work in the process?

Maybe it was a way to commune with my ancestors, who did the same thing on fancy occasions. The formal tablecloth and silverware I began fussing with, even though they were inherited, were passed down from my mother's grandmother and couldn't have been less Jewish. But I'd forgotten how much I appreciated them. The linen was so cool and smooth to touch. There were four different styles of spoon, each a slightly different shape and probably designed for some dish no one ate anymore, like turtle soup. I found I could cocoon with the beautiful things my mother had arranged to give to me after she died, and I wished she were around to see me taking so much pleasure in them on Shabbat.

Until I remembered the part about not driving. The idea of giving it up for twenty-four hours was alarming, since the outside world—a strip mall anchored by Albertson's—was two miles away, and what good was it anyway, since I couldn't carry money? The basics of weekend life became alluring precisely because I couldn't have them. I couldn't go out for dinner and a movie. I couldn't lift weights at the gym. I certainly could not attend opening night of the National Western Stock Show—the largest rodeo in the West. Just because I couldn't, I longed for the media party at the National Western Club bar, where tiny fillet mignon burgers were served with buttery rolls and high-end booze. But I tried to keep an open mind. Jews *adore* the Sabbath, greeting it as a bride.

Soon after sunset, I pulled the fish out of the pan, summoned the children, poured the wine, and said the blessings. It was also proper, said the *Code,* to bless the children—praying that they turn out like the Jewish matriarchs: Sarah, Rebecca, Rachel, and Leah, although I wasn't all that sure about Leah, having read up on her story, as Rabbi Rami had suggested.

May you be like Leah. May your father trick you into marriage with a man who loves your much-prettier younger sister a lot more than he even likes you. May you somehow overcome those cross-eyes and barren ovaries of yours, and soldier on.

I settled on: *May you both be like the women of the Torah, who were brave, smart, and loving.*

"We love you too, Ma," they said, with their mouths full of challah.

It was possible to glow in the reflected light of my family all together in one room, exemplifying the Jewish principle that home is holier than the synagogue. Gus had a Gatorade mustache left over from afternoon snack, Coco had fishnet tights, Eric had my best interests at heart. More than that, he found me entertaining and took me out on dates.

I realized that Friday night walks had once been a Chotzinoff family tradition. I always got to my father's on Friday in time for dinner, and then we'd go for a long walk up Broadway or across West 57th Street. I would take his arm in the old-fashioned way, and we always stopped at jewelry store windows to look at huge rubies and sapphires, which was his idea of swell, not mine. Lest things get boring, he pointed out all the obvious prostitutes.

I started out on foot to the synagogue, under a moonless sky. I walked fast, like a Manhattanite covering forty blocks between Lincoln Center and drinks with friends. Twenty years ago, I could look forward to wild flirtation on a Friday night—or maybe a record exec would just happen to be out there in the crowd. Now what was the draw? Cookies in the social hall. How did I ever get mixed up with a building that contained a social hall?

It was too dark to see my feet. Behind me was an eight-thousand-acre open space full of deer and elk, the traditional foods of mountain lions. Around here, elementary school kids are taught how to deal with mountain lions: Wave your hands above your head! Make noise, but no eye contact. Don't run—they love to chase things! A bear scavenged garbage up and down this road all summer. By now he could be gone, but then maybe not. And what about those Dobermans who run loose at night?

Whatever else they had to put up with, the Orthodox Jews of Crown Heights didn't have to deal with this.

Eric and the kids pulled up next to me in the minivan.

"The service starts in two minutes," he said. "You'll never make it on foot." I opened the passenger door and got in.

"I guess you'll have to be my *Shabbes goy*," I said.

"How about your *Shabbes goy*-toy?" he asked. Ah, Shabbat sex. Such a blessing.

On Saturday, I stayed home trying to enjoy a break from life itself, but the family glow was missing. All three of my nuclear family members went ice-skating—renting skates with actual cash—got into complicated scheduling discussions on the phone, and drove to a party at the fire department. I sat on the couch with a crossword puzzle. Eric found this irritating, as well he might. Who would have thought Shabbat was a selfish thing moms did while dads drove kids around?

In my limited experience, Jewish kids could be cuckoo—tearing around the social hall as if this were an ADD convention. Maybe this was an ancestral reaction to sedentary Shabbats through the ages. Like so many other things, it reminded me of Laura Ingalls Wilder, even though the people she wrote about couldn't have been more Christian. Early in the *Little House* series, Pa tells his own grandfather's story of an endless Sabbath. The adults sat around doing nothing, while three young boys itched to escape. Finally they snuck out and went sledding—right past the open door where their father was snoring in his straight-backed chair. It appeared to be an almost universal urge.

The hell with it. I went to Wal-Mart and bought some duct tape.

I FINISHED *Teach Yourself to Read Hebrew* and began tutoring with Ellen Diesenhof, who taught me to read the first half page of my *haftarah*. Congregation Beth Evergreen continued to audition rabbis. Three candidates visited in three weeks, and I made a point of attending every service. Whoever got the job would be my spiritual leader during the summer leading up to my bat mitzvah, and I wanted a good one. Yet I had a sinking feeling the board was planning to hire a woman I immediately nicknamed The Shrieker, even though a lot of congregants loved her operatic voice. I didn't think it was a good sign that she'd shown us a bunch of cheesy New Age dance moves to perform while saying the evening blessings. I had come to expect this musical schism at Jewish services—the major key, feel-good music, sung in English, duking it out with the ancient, feel-bad-but-then-redeemed songs, most in incomprehensible Hebrew. I knew what I liked, and I got more of it from the next rabbi prospect. Jamie Arnold—my second Rabbi Jamie!—came from Buffalo, New York; had spent time in a Buddhist Monastery in Nepal; gave succinct, Rami-esque sermons that made me sit up straighter in my chair; and had been a musician before becoming a rabbi. His wife, Marti, was a rebellious wisecracker and mother of three.

Rabbis and their families were required to take the helm at synagogues, and it wasn't easy. There was no way to be best friends with everyone. Every single accomplishment had to be done in committee. You had to get used to taking phone calls at home, to handling intercongregant spats, to rushing off to the hospital for hysterectomies, new babies, and deaths. I'd noticed the strain could make rabbis imperious, or cold. The Arnolds weren't. Almost immediately, Marti and I talked about produce— I warned her how bad it would be here compared to the fertile fields and brimming grocery stores of western New York. She told me her youngest daughter, Michaela, was going through the dreaded pink phase, and that whenever Marti got upset about it, Jamie would sing her a song called "Children of Feminists Always Love Barbie."

MY FATHER CAME out of his coma and tried to talk around his breathing tube, but couldn't. He hadn't eaten in almost a week.

"Do you know what happened?" I asked.

He shook his head.

"Do you know you were unconscious?"

He shook his head and then began to pull against the ties that were holding his hands down. I untied one, and he pointed to his foot.

"Foot?" No. "Sock?" No. "Sole? Soul?" No.

Then he pointed to a doctor walking down the hall.

"Doctor? Do you need to see a doctor?" No. "A nurse?" No. He got more and more frustrated. When Marina came in, she got it instantly: shoe, man—Schumann had been playing on the radio.

They took the breathing tube out after four days and sent a speech therapist over to teach him how to eat. My sister Jenny came to visit and pronounced: "He's ready to die. He's tired of living. He's so sick. They should just let him go."

Who was *they*?

He dozed all day, thrashing restlessly. His broken ribs made it excruciating to breathe. He ate little amounts of mush. I was delegated to ask him: "Do you want this to be over? Do you want to die?"

"No!" he said, and got angry enough to heal according to his own plan. Typical. My father had wrecked his own health with singular focus and now there was none left. But rather than accept it, he turned to wild fantasies of eternal life. He asked the ER doctor on a date, planned a trip back east, and insisted on wearing a massive Rolex watch that hung around his bony wrist. The fact was, he really didn't believe in death. It happened to other people.

I read Coco's *Etz Chayim*, the five books of Moses, at my father's bedside as he slept, taking notes. It's natural for a Jew to write commentaries on all the texts, and my middle-aged memory needed a sort of shorthand:

—*Moses walks up a mountain, sees God as a burning bush and is terrified. God calls: Moses! Moses! (Just like my great-grandmother, he says everything twice.) With a dry mouth, Moses replies, Hineini! God says he picked Moses to free the Jews from slavery. Moses says, They'll never believe me if I tell them I got this message from you. God says, How about I give you a staff that turns into a snake and a hand that turns scaly white? That should get their attention. Moses says, Please, I don't want to do this, I'm not a good talker. So use your brother, Aaron, God says. He's slick.*

—The earliest Jews worshiped God "in the wilderness." They don't much now. When did that stop? In general, Jews don't pay much attention to the outdoors; there aren't even many Hebrew words to describe it. Joanne says: "We're lousy at nature, but great at punishments." A lot of Jews don't even like dogs.

—The Egyptians don't believe anything Moses says. Plagues follow. Soot that becomes a skin infection. Eczema in the land. Look, God says, I could have killed all you people but I didn't. I wanted you to be alive in order to see how powerful I am. Boom! Thunder and hail! Those who believe take their stock inside, but most of the cattle die, just like they do in Wyoming during a blizzard.

I had pictured Moses as played by Charlton Heston—craggy and grand, an excellent hiker. But the text changed my mind. At 80, with a speech impediment, Moses received messages from God and found them more disturbing than miraculous. It often seemed as if no one wanted to hear what he had to say.

I had known a guy like him.

We both lived in Berkeley in 1978. Patients were pouring from mental institutions out onto the street. Crazy people were everywhere. They were a lot like us street vendors—we ate the same things, drank at the same places, and kept the same schedule. Most of them panhandled in our territory, and we lived by a loose tithing system. If I'd already earned twenty bucks that day, I gave one dollar to the first mentally ill person I saw.

But it was disconcerting the way they snuck up on me, how I'd look up from my table to see their sunburnt faces much too close, their bodies crisscrossed with lines of grime. And boy, were they upset—bedeviled by miseries no one else could see or feel.

Crooked Woman, whose body was twisted and always dressed in black, visited me every day. She was about thirty, and communicated only in song. Her hand would clamp down on my shoulder. "I don't want to start a five-alarm fire," she'd sing into my face, "just a flame in your heart!"

This didn't faze my vendor friend Heather. She'd remove Crooked Woman's hand, saying, "This is *my* body, not yours. You don't get to touch me unless I say so. You go back outside now." It had a calming effect.

Crooked Woman worked the same block as Cosmic Debris. (We named him for a Frank Zappa song.) He was emaciated, with long grey hair, and wore a toga made from a dirty chenille bedspread. They said he used to be a professor at Berkeley but got caught up in the acid tests, and now his mind was stuck in a series of tape loops. First, he'd make a kind of whoop/beep noise, as if to say, "Message out-coming." And then he'd repeat a piece of information. Things like: "The frequency of footfall on the pavement is directly relative to department output." Or, "The Pythagorean theorem takes triangles for granted." Or something simple, with an echo of doom: "Look out. Look out. Look out."

We stayed out of his way because we respected him as the patriarch of the street. Moses's people must have thought the same about him. *Here he comes again, with his warnings of frogs and plagues. Should we listen this time?* Coz stationed himself at his corner, transmitting his messages, until someone came out and made him move or chickened out and summoned Dan Dial, the polite gay policeman.

Coz spent every day trying to tell us things we didn't want to hear. He was good at intuition, but bad at explanation. He could have used an Aaron to speak to the crowd. What must he have thought when he woke up in the morning with another crazy message to convey, not able to turn down the assignment?

A woman in our Melton class, Reney Lorditch, had a simple explanation for every religious visionary since time began: "Another schizophrenic changes history."

Moses got me thinking almost as much as Jacob, that charming but manipulative teenager, who was anything but crazy. Rabbi Baskin had told us the story several years earlier. Ever since then, it has reminded me of my nephew Nick. Nick was two when my sister Jenny broke up with his father, Chuck. Chuck had every intention of being a good dad, but he often ended up in jail, and was always surprised to find himself there. He'd get pulled over for a simple thing like speeding, but it would turn out there was a warrant for his arrest because he hadn't paid the last speeding fine. Oh, and he dealt a little pot. And did a little drunk driving.

He had a stock response: "It's a hell of a thing to happen to *me*." Jenny and I used to blow off steam by imitating him. But she was in her early twenties, and not entirely ready to be a single mother.

At the time, I had a relatively stable marriage, and Nick spent a lot of time at my house. I was dying to have a child of my own, but it wasn't working, and I probably spoiled Nick. But he was so self-sufficient, so interested in life, so smart. Sometimes I'd check on him late at night and he would wake up and smile at me in the dark.

"Go back to sleep," I'd say, but then I'd have to wait until morning to see him again, so we'd start up another hour or so of conversation. Jenny called me Auntie Overstimulation.

Nick started to fall apart when he was fourteen. He was smarter than his father, we thought, but he'd learned the family methods. He rode his Vespa through downtown Denver in the middle of the night, got stopped for speeding, and had dope in his pocket. He'd been an actor for years, but now he couldn't stop arguing with his performing arts school teachers and was almost always suspended, anyway. Being constantly stoned didn't help. It was a hell of a thing to happen to *him*, but he thought he could get around it if he were smart enough. He definitely had a few ideas. Remembering this, it was no big stretch to think of Jacob, to compare and contrast.

—*Jacob was a twin, born second, who came into the world holding on to his brother's heel. He was out to get his brother Esau, who lived up to his name, which means "hairy." Esau was a hunter and a herder—a manly man, but dumb as a post. Jacob hung out in his mother's tent, learning how to get what he wanted. One day when Esau came back hungry from the hunt, Jacob offered him "a mess of potage" in exchange for his "birthright"—a bowl of lentil soup for his entire inheritance. Jacob must have been one hell of a salesman.*

One day, Nick asked Jenny to give him some money, but she pointed out he'd already spent his allowance. After throwing a classic teen tantrum, he allowed anger to bring out his creativity.

He walked across the street and robbed a bank for six hundred dollars. It was easy.

—Jacob was sarcastic and self-referential, but his parents loved him and everyone else put up with him. It was simple to trick Esau again—this time out of his own father's blessing, which was even more important than an inheritance in those days.

Nick was only fourteen. Not a seasoned bank robber. The surveillance cameras caught his every move, and not only that, he'd filled out a loan application. They busted him right away, and Jenny got a lawyer.

—Jacob's parents disowned him. Enough was enough. He walked away from his father's camp, carrying nothing but a skin of water.

As Auntie Overstimulation, I had no authority over Nick or his life. But I thought he needed protection. So I sewed him a quilt that was black with small explosions of color in it, and for the quilting lines I sewed Jacob's Ladders, one on top of the other.

"There's a story to this quilt," I said. "And you just let me know when you want to hear it."

I didn't want to freak him out with religious talk.

"Cool," he said.

I tried to talk to him about robbing the bank, but it was as if he was too young or distractible to comprehend what he'd done, although he did cry a little. Only a few months earlier, he'd had grandiose plans, mostly involving money-making. But at this point he seemed powerless and small. The zoot suit I'd bought him during his swing-dancing phase had become too big. He didn't seem to understand cause and effect. His lawyer being the best money could buy, he didn't spend much time in juvenile detention.

—Jacob walked through the empty desert in a rage—what had he done wrong but use the brains God gave him? On the third night, he fell asleep with his head on a stone. It wasn't a restful situation—more like a dark campground full of raccoons. Jacob ground his teeth in his sleep and had vivid dreams.

After his release, Nick went to work as a trapeze instructor at a Mexican resort. On days off, he took the bus into town and walked the alleys, using one of his only reliable Spanish phrases—*"para nariz"*—to search for cocaine. The new drug was a rush, but also, he came to think, the missing piece of his brain chemistry. When he came home to Denver, good old Chuck, his hopeless, helpless father, who survived on visions of success in a sales job, introduced him to crack, and together, in between clumsy illegal scamming and sleepless weeks, they had visions of other worlds.

—Jacob dreamed of a ladder rising into the sky. At first, it seemed like the shortcut to heaven he'd been looking for. But the ladder was crowded with angels—big, noisy, blue-collar angels with huge wings. They got Jacob's attention.

Jenny found his car in front of a crack house in a skin-crawling neighborhood, slashed its tires, and waited. When Nick finally emerged, she gave him a choice: jail or rehab. A few days later, they flew to a recovery ranch in Riverside, California, and Jenny gave him up. During his detox month, he saw visions of God—in water, under his pillow, inside a closet. One morning he became Jesus and tried to walk across the surface of a swimming pool.

—When Jacob woke up, his stone pillow was wet with dew. The ladder and the angels were gone. He was scared and stunned and wrapped in warmth at the same time—whatever had messed with him

in the night was mother and father at the same time. The Torah says he was "shaken." He hadn't been a particularly emotional guy before. He had done what he wanted, but he could see that was about to change.

"Surely the Lord is in this place," he said, "and I did not know it."

After a month of detox, Nick was sent to Sober Living by the Sea in Newport Beach. He lived in a house with three other recovering addicts, was given an Albertson's debit card to buy groceries, went to AA meetings, and rode a rusty cruiser bike around town, which had its share of street people, drunks, and drug addicts. He was allowed to have visitors, but only by prior written permission. The only clearance I could get was for the exact twenty-four hours of my next planned Shabbat. I felt a little strange telling Nick about the boundaries I'd set for myself, but he had plenty himself and seemed to understand. Neither of us, for instance, was allowed to carry money. For me, it would constitute work. For him, it would constitute temptation—there were lots of illegal substances for sale in Newport.

The town was damp and full of cheesy nautical restaurants, and I felt very comfortable there. Until Nick materialized out of the fog, I hadn't really been sure he was still alive. He was, but he was different—agitated from anti-psychotic drugs, and fat, though he'd always been ropy and muscled from all that trapeze and all those drugs. He laughed and patted his belly. An eating disorder was not going to be one of his problems. The weight was on its way off. He talked fast, brimming with AA aphorisms and high as a kite on what recovering addicts call The Pink Cloud.

"What'll you do when you're tempted to start smoking crack again?" I asked.

"It'll never happen. I don't even need to think about it."

"What does your sponsor say?"

"He says it'll happen."

"Listen to him," I said, feeling ineffectively bossy, exactly the way my mom felt about me when I was Nick's age. We went out for Mexican. Nick talked breathlessly about the letter he was writing Chuck, who was locked up once again. He wanted to tell Chuck to recover.

"If he doesn't, I can't see him anymore," he explained.

"I wouldn't think so," I said.

"But I want him to get into treatment."

Halfway through fajitas, I remembered the Shabbat blessings. The Reconstructionist prayer book we use at Beth Evergreen has many versions. I knew I could tweak them to match the situation, but I didn't say them aloud.

Blessed are you, caretaker of the universe, who protects young addicts and puts them a thousand miles away from their fathers and helps them to stay straight, one day at a time, as they like to say.

After dinner, we went to an AA meeting full of kids whose parents could afford to send them to three-month rehab in one of the most expensive cities in the country.

"Before I came here, I was a crack whore who lived under a bush most of the time," said a girl in low-slung, two-hundred-buck jeans, more embarrassed at having gained twenty pounds than at having lived under the bush. "I still don't like it here," she said. "After a few days I called my mother and I'm like, 'Please let me come home.' She said no! She never said no to me before."

When it got to be Nick's turn, he jumped out of his chair and said, "My aunt made me a quilt! And I still have it! And here she is!"

The young addicts were in a collective terrible mood, disillusioned and sarcastic. Ready to give up and use. At the same time, no one flinched at the mention of God. Nick had stopped minding at all.

"They said I needed to accept a power greater than myself, and I had no problem with that," he said. "I mean, it could be God or it could be a sock. What do I care? I figure anything is more powerful than me at this point."

We sat on a dock with our feet hanging out over the water, talking comfortably about what the rest of our family found uncomfortable, reading aloud from the Big Book, which I accepted as the week's Torah portion.

"I talk to God," I said, "but he doesn't talk to me."

"Yeah, well, he talked to me all the time when I was getting clean," Nick said, "and it was fucking terrifying. He was telling me I would die if I didn't pay attention. And I had to pay attention, because he was everywhere."

—*Angels hovered around Jacob for the rest of his life, and they weren't anything like the sheltering angels sold in Christian gift shops. As the Torah progresses, he goes back out into the world, gets not one but two wives, and becomes responsible for an entire tribe of people. For the rest of his life, he has nightmares—one an all-night wrestling match with another big, bad angel. He emerges with an injured hip and a new name: Israel.*

His prayer changes, from "God, give me what I want, and stop scaring me," to "I want to do your will, and how can I if you kill me?"

It took a lot of celestial boxing matches, but eventually he decided to care about other people in the same way he cared about himself, to accept all the interdependence that comes with family.

I wanted this for Nick. For the moment, he had started to care about dogs, whose simple needs were easy to fill. He took a minimum-wage job as a kennel tech, and liked it, so far.

"I DREAMT YOU were here," my father said. He'd been moved to a rehab hospital to get strong enough, after lying in bed for weeks, to walk.

"I *was* here," I said. "You just kept falling asleep."

"I might be going to die," he said conversationally.

"Are you afraid?"

"Why should I be afraid to die? I'm not afraid. I'm pissed. It's the lack of continuity that pisses me off."

I left because it was Friday afternoon—countdown to my next stab at a structured Shabbat. I came home and began trying to defrost a large brisket in a small microwave. The upcoming soiree with God was making me frantic.

"Uh, should we just leave you *alone* so you can do your Shabbat thing?" Eric asked, which wasn't the point at all. What I really wanted was for him to enter the house in Tevye the Dairyman style: take off his leather cap, stained by honest toil; call for a basin in which to wash his brawny arms; and then bless all the females in the house, from small to big. But he didn't, and the dinner wasn't coming together at all, and neither was my role as a wife and mother whose value was a price beyond rubies.

So we went to the neighborhood sports bar for beer and *trayf* cheeseburgers, and the next morning we went snowboarding. The Adventure Rabbi had called this a fine, if Reform, way to spend the Sabbath. All kinds of driving and striving were involved, and you absolutely can't do a downhill sport without carrying money, and plenty of it. This is the land of the seventy-buck lift ticket, the eight-buck hot cocoa.

Eric and I went up past timberline to a knob where the wind exposed bare sheets of ice. Getting off the chairlift, I fell so hard my helmet bounced off the ground. But once we got back into the trees, we flew around in deep drifts and I didn't feel I had to keep up with Eric or anyone else. I lay on my back and let the snow fall on my face, appreciating that God's creation gets your attention when it's extreme. Was it at all holy to lie there until I got cold and then ride as fast as I could down to the lodge for a hot drink? Is it any less holy than laying out a special white tablecloth and sitting a lot, in order to rest? Was white snow its own kind of tablecloth?

When ski school was over, Gus came sliding down the mountain toward us, a smile on her little red-cheeked six-year-old face, with all the top teeth missing.

"Can we go up again?" she said.

In the car on the way home, I tested the afternoon against my favorite Shabbat rule: Quit rushing and schlepping for a day. Snowboarding for the sheer joy of sliding downhill, without worrying about traffic or lift lines or the price of a burrito, wasn't exactly tradition. But it could count as returning to our roots as Jews worshiping God in the wilderness. Down in Denver, Orthodox families were spending the afternoon walking sedately around Sloan's Lake, but, as my father loved to say, *things change.* I decided it was okay to make my own rules, and in fact I had no choice. Except that I hated rules. So fine—I'd have damn few. Here they are:

> Friday at sunset, stop doing what makes you crazy, such as writing things down, remembering, planning, messing with other people's destinies, stirring the pot, begging for feedback, and doing more than one thing at once.
>
> Light candles. Sharpen knives. Cook something that smells good. If you can't, crush a piece of oregano between your fingers.
>
> Creating is fine. Achieving is prohibited.

ON PURIM, MY family and I dressed up like Gypsies to help at the synagogue children's carnival. I sat behind a sign that read: "Madame Chotzinoff, Palm Readings and Fortunes." A Gypsy is not a Jew, but plenty of Judaism centers around the heavy foreshadowing of dreams and bizarrely supernatural explanations for things that could be accounted for with logic. Jacob turns into Israel by wrestling with an angel. A hundred years ago, Eastern European girls who lost their minds were said to be possessed by *dybbuks,* voracious lost souls who encouraged their victims to say shocking things in public, to be loud, sluttish, and unapologetic. No one put these girls on trains to Vienna for visits with Dr. Freud, although a rabbi miracle worker might have been consulted. Something in my personality made me able to accept these fancies, perhaps because they had a touch of the wiseass about them, or because I'd read so much Isaac Bashevis Singer, who writes about hallucinations in a matter-of-fact way.

I was comfortable suspending belief enough to see the future in small hands covered with ballpoint doodlings, and the children who received my spooky prophecies left slightly disoriented. I liked to stare at their hands long and hard before allowing myself to say a word, because it got us both in the mood.

Your grades may not be that good, but you're going to kick ass in law school and join a high-powered Jewish frat and become a senator . . . My goodness, could you really be going to work with killer whales? How will you have time for your six kids—three sets of twins . . . It's simple. You will be a great artist, making paintings big enough to fit on the sides of buildings.

For my father, I saw visitors from the east.

Three years ago, Aunt Cookie would have been the obvious choice. She'd spent her whole life catering to him, picking every bone out of the fish fillets she cooked for him, pleading with him to quit smoking, going with him on his hair-raising hurricane watching trips. When she married Uncle Herb, it got complicated. Understandably, he didn't want to share Aunt Cookie with my father. Sometimes Dad and Uncle Herb united long enough to quit speaking to Chotzie. More often, they argued with each other. Wagner vs. Mozart—and Uncle Herb, being an orchestra conductor, more than held his own. Instant gratification vs. scrimping for the future. Even Top-Siders vs. flip-flops. But Aunt Cookie died in 2002, and it was Uncle Herb who decided to visit, with his new girlfriend, Sylvia Davis, an opera singer.

What gossip! Dad came alive. When Sylvia arrived, with her long silver hair and movie-star face, he slapped his teeth into his mouth and started trying to steal her from Uncle Herb, who, at seventy-eight, took it as a compliment. The three of them sat for two days in the rehab hospital room, reminiscing about arguments they'd had with Chotzie and Pauline, the age-old Mozart vs. Wagner, and whatever medical procedures might get my father back on his feet and into the belly of the family.

First of all, he had to learn to walk again.

"You need to really *try* to get better," Uncle Herb said. "Promise me you'll put some effort into it. I've talked to the physical therapists and they want to check you into a nursing home for more rehab. Not forever! After that, you go home. I want you to promise me you'll try."

"Promise me you'll try," Sylvia echoed, smiling flirtatiously. Dad stopped talking about croaking for the moment.

"They're going to kick me out!" my father said a few days later. "Christ, that girlfriend of Herb's is attractive. I wonder how he did it."

A buzzer went off from somewhere inside the tangle of wires connected to his body. His heart rate sank. Nurses pushed me out of the way and started injecting drugs into the IV. Five minutes later, Dad was "normal" again.

"They're a nice bunch of broads," Dad observed. "The blond one, Nola, has a kid at home but no man in the picture."

"Nola" was the name of an old song, and when Nola the nurse came in to check up, Dad sang it to her.

She said her grampa used to sing that song for her. She began to cry.

Dad never liked being lumped in with other people's grampas—it had always been a dubious way to arrange dates with beautiful nurses. This time, though, he didn't complain.

Marina and I set out on a tour of nursing homes. At a place that billed itself as the highest-rated facility in Colorado, we were interviewed by a tense woman in a shiny black wig—was she Orthodox?—who fumbled in her desk as if feeling for a bottle of bourbon. Following her through the halls, we kept bumping into silent old people strapped into wheelchairs.

"I would like my lunch now," one of the marooned old men said. Employees walked right past him on their way to bingo, balloon animals, and Make Your Own Leprechaun Day. The old people were crowded into tiny rooms with roommates they'd never met before, just a very few family photographs arranged on little squares of wall.

"And you can see our lovely carpets and brand new bedspreads, I'm sure," Shiny Wig Woman said. "And how *about* these curtains?"

"We absolutely can't do that to him," Marina said.

Even if we tried to, he wouldn't let us. He was too smart and devious not to plot an escape. He'd never had any trouble persuading people that it was up to them to make him feel good because he currently felt bad. Hence the dozen or more doctors who'd agreed to prescribe him paregoric—a sort of liquid opium—for his stomach ailments, or whatever they actually were. He'd have no trouble talking some nurse into pirating his Suburban and taking him away at dead of night.

Next stop was a high-rise, Soviet-style concrete facility that had recently reopened after having been shut down by the Department of Health. It was part of a big national chain, a supposedly soulless managed-care institution. Instead of lovely carpets, it had worn linoleum floors and flickering fluorescent lights, but the rooms were large and private, and in the physical therapy room we found three beautiful women just waiting for someone to rehabilitate.

"Does your father need a diabetic diet?" the director asked. "Even if he does, we won't make him. At this age, people should get to eat what they want."

"Can he wheel into the kitchen and cook himself a few fried eggs?" Marina asked.

"Sure. Why not?"

The director was a radical—he loved his job. He loved walking from room to room, getting into philosophical conversations with the people he called "guests." If he could ever own his own nursing home, he said, he would anchor the ground floor with a chapel on one end and a bar on the other. Services every day, happy hour every night.

Unfortunately, the Soviet nursing home had no way to get my Dad to dialysis, and without that, he'd die. The situation called for pointless worrying. And God-muttering.

Hello, Mother. Thank you for everything. Thank you for my dog, Gumbo, who reads my mind and never interrupts these talks; for mechanical pencils; and moments of clarity—looking out the window, watching a blizzard move toward me from the mountains. And thanks for making me the sort of Jew who understands that you actually didn't

ask me to believe that you moved this particular blizzard to this par-
ticular mountain, only to pay attention to the look of the sky.

Help me stay away from those fatty Boar's Head sandwiches at the
gas station as a way of reminding me that food is sacred fuel, not some
twisted drug. Help me help Marina move Dad into that new nursing
home. She shouldn't have to do everything just because she's his room-
mate. I should go down to town, but I need to be with you more than I
need to be with him. Help me pick up the phone, anyway. But what if
he hates the new place and wants me to come get him? The altitude up
here would kill him, and his kidneys would fail, and the thing is, I don't
want to rescue him anyway—it's too hard. Help me pick up the phone,
Mother, even though I don't believe you work that way and I agree with
Marina that football players who thank God for every touchdown are
ridiculous. Help me make the call.

I didn't. Marina and Ryan took up the slack. That night, they
brought over the forbidden, homey dinner Dad requested: a
concoction of crab with a sherry-cream sauce. He had already
started telling the nurses the saga of finding the songwriter
Johnny Mercer in a faint at a night club and reviving him with
the bottle of smelling salts he just happened to have on hand.
When I was little, I used to open it up sometimes, to see if I
could make myself more awake. It was a salty, fishy smell—for-
tuitously similar to caviar.

My father died sometime during that night at the new nursing home, but he still hadn't signed a Do Not Resuscitate order,
and the paramedics pounded his chest for a full thirty minutes.
He came creaking back to life, and they shipped him back to
the ICU.

Marina and I found him unconscious again, with his hands tied and a tube down his throat. His brain had been starved for oxygen for a half hour or more. We knew this meant his circuits were burnt to a crisp. When we squeezed his hand, he didn't squeeze back. His eyes were half open, but all we could see were the whites—when a nurse touched his eyeball with a Q-tip, he didn't flinch. Marina found the place in his will that talked about a persistent vegetative state. He didn't want to be kept alive at that point.

The next day, Jenny, Marina, and I moved into our father's hospital room to sit with him while he died his final death. Marina brought his pocket flask filled with bourbon. They took out his breathing tube and shut down every machine but the heart rate monitor, and the doctor came in to explain that he would die gradually and never in the slightest pain. Her hair was pinned up in a bun, but she took it down and shook it. We noticed her expensive pumps and perfect legs.

"Of course," Jenny said. "He wouldn't dream of dying for anyone else."

All day long the green numbers descended. Near sunset, we ran out of Dad stories to tell. All three of us were tired. We became quiet and took turns holding his hand. A chaplain came in, which Dad wouldn't have liked, but we were nice to her and asked her about herself, and he would have approved of that.

Finally he gave three deep sighs—the agonal breathing that comes with death. It was a contented sound. The doctor came in, closed his eyes, and gave him a kiss on the forehead, as if he were still an irresistibly good-looking man.

I rested my forehead on my father's arm. Though he had stopped breathing, some part of him was getting ready to move. As a Jew, I believe only simple things about death. Death means it's over. Time to turn into compost. But I'd also read Jewish folk tales that referred to the Next World. I had no interest in trying to believe in that, but I enjoyed the concept, especially where Dad was concerned. He was on the move, even if it was only from one hemisphere of my brain to another.

How strange that his skin was warm and the position we were in was so familiar, no different than when I fell asleep against his shoulder in the front seat of the Impala. Once he had been the unmistakable adult in my life, and I had been the child. This was when I was little and didn't have to think about where we were going.

Hineini

SEPTEMBER 24, 2005

6:00 A.M.

When you're young, you have desire. When you're old, you have a plan. The dogs and I are up before anyone else.

I tell myself nothing can go wrong at my bat mitzvah. I have everything I need, even a color scheme. The paper plates and cups, the tablecloth and the irises, and even the flowers on my white dress, are all yellow and blue. Matchy-matchy, I know, but I never went to prom in high school and today is as close as I'll get. I'm my own date. I'll try not to blame myself if I screw this up, because it was the best I could do.

I miss my parents. They should be here to take care of me, to soak up the overwhelming details. My mother would have sent out invitations, gone to the party store, fielded calls from the out of towners arriving at the airport. My father would have been cooking—chopped liver for seventy-five, capons, herring, and matzo balls. He would have invited his friends. He would have been proud.

"The thing is," I told Rabbi Arnold yesterday, "my parents actually wouldn't be doing any of that stuff. They were wonderful, but they weren't into religion. And there aren't any out-of-town relatives. My father might not even have come. He wouldn't have told his friends. I'm forty-seven—I can handle this without my mother, but even if I couldn't, she died in 1997."

"The people you miss are in some way real," he said, "even if you made them up."

I like this new rabbi a lot. The Congregation Beth Evergreen board was unable to make a deal with The Shrieker, and, on the same day my father died, they hired Rabbi Jamie Arnold. He and his family have been here for two months. We've drunk beer together at the free lake concerts, discussed the merits of Home Depot plumbing supplies, and, last Friday night, when he asked someone to sing something, I did one verse of an old-time bluegrass hymn, and he already knew it. He listens to a lot of blues and a little Charlie Parker. He doesn't flinch if you call him by his first name. His daughter Michaela invited Gus to spend the night, and he lent her a T-shirt that read *Got Rabbi?* as a nightie.

But he's eleven years younger than I am—not the same thing as a parent. And he shouldn't be.

Both my mother and father have plaques on the new *yahrzeit* wall at the back of the synagogue. On the month of each of their deaths, a light will go on next to their names. I bought them these few square inches of eternity because both my parents' ashes are packed in boxes about the size of a loaf of bread, one sitting in a closet, the other on a living room shelf. Years ago, Jenny and I talked about immortalizing them in a much more visible way. I remembered walking near a pond at the Bel-Air Hotel with my mother and seeing a baby swan floating asleep, its head under its wing.

"Oh!" my mother said. "I could sleep that way forever!" A bronze swan in a garden, we thought, would be the perfect tribute to her. As long as we were at it, we thought we'd commission a bronze duck for Dad, who wasn't even sick at the time. We picked a duck because Dad loved them. They lived in his style, swimming around lazily, often paired up romantically. True, he'd been known to hunt and eat ducks, but that didn't lessen his affection, and he liked quacking back to them so much he made a point of sitting near bodies of water in case one or two should swim by. We asked if he'd mind sharing a space with our mother, though they hadn't been married since 1964.

"All right with me," he said, "if you think it's all right with her."

But we never built the duck and swan garden because we were too transient. Both of us had acquired the habit of moving every few years. And now I want to be formally reminded of my parents in a public place. I wonder if either of my sisters will notice the plaques when they come to synagogue today.

If they don't, my Jewish friends will. We jump into action when someone dies. Less than a week after my father died, the members of my *shul* convened in my living room for a short and pointed service. We read from Edna St. Vincent Millay and Nachman of Bratslav, who said, "All this life is a very narrow bridge. The important thing is to not be afraid." I knew some of the people there; others came out of respect. A handful of Christian firefighters came, too—like the Jews, they appreciated the protocol for honoring a man they'd never met.

They asked if I wanted to say something about my father, as few of them had ever met him. For once, I couldn't come up with a story. A sort of stage fright came up from inside me and scared me for a moment. But then I showed them a picture from my fourth birthday. I was wearing a paper tiara and Dad was helping me cut the cake. We'd repeated this shot when I turned forty, and Dad looked almost exactly the same—the aviator sunglasses and the ratty old button-down shirt rolled up high above his biceps, his hair still black and slicked down with a comb. That told the story reasonably well.

Everyone brought something sweet. For the first time in my life, I felt as if I would never run out of dessert.

A few weeks later, my sisters and I had a party for Dad at the Denver Press Club. Hundreds of people came. The gossip columnists ran items, the obituary writers sank their teeth into his story. His old friend Sam remembered accompanying my father as he piloted, and crashed, a small rented plane. Coco, who had been afraid to play her cello for Dad while he was alive, played at the party. Gloria Steinem looked at all the people and said aloud what we all thought—that we'd all be lucky to draw this big a crowd just by dying.

"Really," she said. "It's fan-fucking-tastic."

Clearly, Dad had been rehearsing this last achievement all his life. We ate and drank and then it was done, except for the kaddish prayer I was supposed to say for him every day for eleven months. The kaddish is supposed to be for the living, but it didn't entirely do the closure trick for me. I probably should have actively mourned for the prescribed full month because, although my father's body was not just dead but reduced to ashes, some part of him was still around, and it wanted my attention. He talked, a lot more frantically than he had when he was alive, trying to turn my focus back to him. For nearly a month, when running on the treadmill or driving down the mountain, I heard him yakking. *Don't forget me! Don't let anyone else forget me! Tell my stories! Cook my recipes! Never mind* you! *What about* me?

A month was long enough. He began to piss me off. I told Eric I wanted to talk back: to tell my father that I had to practice chanting my *haftarah* and needed him to pipe down. I found myself actually wondering how one gets through to the dead.

Eric went on eBay and bought me a telephone in the shape of a duck—it quacks for incoming calls. The plan was to cement it to a pile of rocks at the farthest edge of my property, so that I could go out there undisturbed and talk to my father.

"Will you settle down?" I planned to say. "I've got it under control. I tell stories about you. No one's going to forget. Anyway, how's the Next World? Have you managed to find any decent rye bread? Have you run into any of the El Morocco showgirls?"

The duck phone helped to calm us both down.

7:00 A.M.

My coming-of-age dress has taken nearly a year to complete, probably because we sewed it by hand, and also because I didn't want the process to end. Last Sunday, I stood in the autumn sun in Joanne's front yard in my underwear as she pinned the last seam.

"Stand up straight," she said. "You have an odd curve."

"Are you accusing me of scoliosis?"

"Absolutely. What have you done with this zipper?"

"Well, I did the best I could," I said, "but I know it doesn't really zip."

Joanne made it zip. She could make anything zip. A storyteller makes her own clothes to separate this world from that, and when I was with her, I was happy in the storytelling world.

We spent the rest of the afternoon attaching *tzitzit* (wool fringes ordered specially from Israel) to the prayer shawl I made out of my gentile great-grandmother's white linen tablecloth. Joanne showed me how to make buttonholes by hand. Who else around here would know a thing like that?

Again I thought of Laura Ingalls Wilder, who finished her own wedding dress the day before her marriage to Almanzo. This scene was the mirror image of that. On the other hand, Joanne and I had decided on sex as the perfect conversational topic for two women making buttonholes, and I don't know if Laura would have dared. Daylight savings time was still in effect, and I stayed until the air got cold, sewing outside under the brittle lilacs.

I hope that having sewn my own seams will make me look presentable. I hope to feel comfortable in my own skin. This is no day for fruitless primping.

8:00 A.M.

My kitchen looks as if it were set up for a church supper. Yesterday, when I was supposed to be helping make food, I sat in a chair having asthma attacks as the women in my life cooked a feast—

my two daughters; my mother-in-law, Betsy; my sister Marina; and her sister-in-law Sarah, a Minnesota atheist so interested in Judaism she came all the way out here to help prepare Middle Eastern treats.

I see power in here I didn't see before. My kitchen has two sets of doors. Wind, dust, mud, and dogs are blowing through. All I have to do to see the grandeur of God is go outside, but God is not all grandness. God is flour and water. God is flowers and water.

It's said that our Jewish God is at least half feminine. They call her the *Shechina*—which seems to mean "dwelling place," or "presence of God in a place," but is also thought to be a goddess-worship word that predates Judaism. We sing well-meaning songs about her on Friday nights, but until recently I thought the whole thing was a fiction arranged to keep women from getting too upset about Judaism's overload of patriarchs.

But a few months after my father died, Eric and I went to Nova Scotia. Nova Scotia is surrounded by salt water, and we went not just to bicycle, but because I miss the ocean. Right away, I got all the non-Colorado weather I wanted—rain, fog, enough humidity to grow fields of purple and blue lupines.

One cold afternoon, we crossed a small channel on a cable ferry. On the far shore, in the middle of nowhere, we found a bakery housed in an old shipbuilding factory. We drank hot tea.

I noticed that someone had painted fishes on the wooden floor—a trail through the twists of the old building. Eric was busy reading the paper, and I began to follow. I went down a staircase into a working bakery with dough machines. Flour dust floated in the air. Big wicker baskets full of homemade bagels sat on the floor. It was a beautiful place that didn't realize how beautiful it was, awash in the smell of salt and hot bread. The path wound across a landing and up a flight of stairs. The stairwell was painted turquoise green. I felt my heart rate go up as I mounted the stairs. At the top, I looked through a large window to a view of endless water. Wavy light seemed to make the floor ripple and rock. The door to the women's bathroom was open behind me, its walls also blue-green, and I went inside, locked the door behind me, and got into the fetal position, shaking, sweating, and crying. There was nothing tangible in the room but a toilet, a sink, and the reflection of water. I allowed the old gypsy in me to interpret what was happening. I had always felt I had a lot to apologize for—that my mistakes would ride me forever. But now this surrounding presence, the ladies room *Shechina*, washed over me and flooded me with acceptance.

I had never considered this side of God—in fact, I didn't understand why anyone was interested in it. I had never trusted revelations either. They had an unsettling habit of fading into Shirley MacLaineism. All that was still true, except that this feeling was so unbelievably pure and fine that I already dreaded the moment it would leave. I was swamped with the unconditional love I didn't believe in.

"Only God can do that," Joanne said, and I hadn't known what she was talking about until now. It took me a long time to finally pee. Luckily, no one knocked on the door.

Finally I went back to our table and finished my tea.

"Excuse me," I said to Eric, who lowered his newspaper. "I had a sort of revelation in the bathroom. I've never been in a room like that before."

"You're talking about a bathroom?"

I made him follow me back along the fish trail. As soon as we hit the second flight of stairs, I began to shake again.

"That's an intense color," he said.

"Do you feel the building shaking? Or is it rocking? It seems to be rocking. Not in an earthquake way," I hastened to add.

"It's very beautiful up here," he said, "especially for a bathroom."

"I don't know how I'm going to explain this. This is New Age hooey, isn't it?"

"I don't know."

"I am at peace," I said.

"Well, good."

We went on with the trip, but sometimes I wished my bike would turn around and lead me back to where I seemed to belong.

Now I watch for God in places where water is running and people are working with things like flour. It isn't as though all women do is cook and clean and wear aprons. I, of all people, should know that. But I still think that if I come face-to-face with God again, this is where she'll be.

9:00 A.M.

Coco keeps me company on the way to the synagogue. Hal Aqua, the cantor, is tuning up in the sanctuary. I have to remind myself that a bat mitzvah is not a gig.

But all summer I daydreamed about the music I would write and the jokes I would tell—a *yiddishe* Tonight Show acted out during the day. My guests would shed glory on me the way they did at the seventh-grade audition for the annual Gilbert and Sullivan operetta,

and again, I would snag the biggest part. I would bake my own challahs and make my own prayer shawl and become such an impres-
sive Hebrew chanter that some impresario would suggest I take my
act on the road and at first I'd say, "Oh, I'm flattered, but I couldn't
possibly," but he'd twist my arm and soon I'd be playing the biggest
temples and religious cabarets on the West Coast.

"It's not really a performance," Rabbi Jamie said. "The music
part is about getting the congregation to go someplace with you.
And *you* don't even really know where it's going. You might end
up singing extra verses, the tempo might suddenly speed up—
you might be loud, you might be soft. All it is, is setting the mood
to pray."

I never know if music will get me in the mood to pray or to
loathe myself, but there's something in it that can move anyone
closer to God, even if they call it something else. Today I don't
have to crawl under the piano and cry the way I used to when I
played at bars, because this won't reflect on me. Or that's what
Jamie says. We will be one voice and all I have to do is blend in.

I rehearsed with Hal last week—the first time I'd done that in
ten years. We learned Jimmy Cliff's "Sitting in Limbo" and Rabbi
Jack Gabriel's version of Bob Marley's "One Love." These reggae
songs strike me as the ultimate *niggunim,* the songs that make you
feel Jewish enough to pray with other Jews, and so what if they
originated with two rastas?

9:30 A.M.

Marina brings me a silver locket with an *R* engraved on it. Inside
is a picture of my dog Gumbo, with his white nose and mis-

matched eyes, one blue, one brown. She fastens it around my neck. People have started to arrive. I'm too nervous to look at them. I sit with my hands in my lap, remembering the first time I came among these people and was shocked at their noisy, irreverent chatter and the way their kids ran loose in the building. This morning, I'm grateful for that. Maybe we'll never have to start the service. But then we do and singing is a great relief, especially the chorus: "Let's get together and feel all right."

I once saw Bob Marley in concert, outside, during a full moon. He ran in place in front of his microphone. I believe this was his way of staying in the mood to pray.

"Give thanks and praise to the One, and we will feel all right."

I find I can rest on this kind of singing, as if it were a platform.

9:45 A.M.

I wrote my own song to take the place of Morning Blessings. My brother-in-law Ryan gave me the idea. Standing in his woodshop one day, I realized that prayer has a lot in common with woodworking. If you don't somehow sand and prime your soul first, if you don't come in contact with how much you long for God, your prayers will roll off your psyche like a bad coat of spray paint. I accomplish this through sweat. When I lift weights, I like to recite Rabbi Rami's Chasidic chant, the one he learned from Sheik Jake the Sufi, who learned it from Reb Zalman—I don't speak aloud or even move my lips, but it works.

Echad Yachid umi Yuchad
Echad Yachid umi Yuchad

The one, every single one,
Each one joined and united in the one.

The song I wrote is called "I'm Alive." With Jamie and Hal singing and playing, it sounds exactly right. By the time I realize the implications—that I may feel like playing music in public again after this, that I actually love to play the piano and sing, and for the first time nothing's wrong with it, that my quavering voice and my three chords are *just fine*—the song is over. My musical family seems to have mellowed along with me. On his last visit, Uncle Herb asked me to consider piano lessons for my kids, "just for the pleasure of it."

10:00 A.M.

Coco comes toward me with my tablecloth prayer shawl. Traditionally, this a role for a parent, but when it comes to Judaism, that's what she's been for me. She helps me remember the blessings and closes the shawl around my shoulders with the clip I bought her last year for Chanukah. Rabbi Jamie says ritual fringes originated near the beginning of Judaism—they were worn to show the rest of the world who we were. After the destruction of the temple, they became more priestly garments, and at a Jewish service everyone in the room is a priest. So he says. I'll pray in this private tent, like so many other Jews. I wonder what my great-grandfather Moshe Baer looked like in his. I wonder what my mystical great-great-grandfather Shnayer Tresskanov looked like in his.

10:15 A.M.

Not having reached the age of bat mitzvah herself, Gus has only a few jobs at this service. She's memorized a poem and invited four of her friends to help her open the Ark of the Torah. They're shy, but impressed with the formality of it all. Rabbi Jamie settles the Torah in my arms. I'm supposed to walk through the congregation while the pick-up klezmer band makes a joyful noise unto the Lord. People are hugging me as I pass, squeezing the Torah scrolls against me. Nancy from the fire department; Tim from winter cycling drills; Tony, who fixes my computer and tells me about Jesus; my dad's old friend Ray, in a proper suit. All these *goyim* have heard me talk about becoming a Jew, but now I'm carrying my faith around in my arms, and there can't be much ambiguity left. It's possible at this point that I'm actually dancing, spinning, with people's faces blurring like they did ten years ago when Eric and I did our wedding dance to a Mexican folk tune called "El Orangutan." Thank God I'm barefoot—if you drop the Torah, it's forty years of bad luck for everyone in this room, and there are so many people here. Not necessarily because of my bat mitzvah, but because the synagogue has exploded with activity in the past few months.

I've spent more and more time inside these walls. Two weeks ago, I was sitting in the hall watching Coco direct tiny kids, of whom Gus was the tallest, during choir practice. Adults in the social hall were acting out a play called "The Trial of Abraham." Downstairs, I heard the big kids singing "Avinu Malkenu." The delivery guy arrived with the kosher pizza, and then Rabbi Jamie came in, covered with drops of white paint—he'd been painting his bathroom and lost track of time. Most of the people who bustled past me had also shown up for Israeli folk dancing, an activity I'd always sworn I would never do. But within minutes I was wringing sweaty, slamming into the synagogue president and the new rabbi and laughing so hard that the instructor had to scream at us, collectively, to shut up and follow directions. There hadn't even been booze, but what was the big deal? My cousin James happened to have come in from L.A., and he turned out to have been a folk dancer from way back. He said the pastime had been invented to help young Zionists get to know each other as they built a new country.

There are *lamed-vavniks* in the room—some of the thirty-six righteous people Rabbi Rami says walk the earth at any given time. The *lamed-vavniks* in Evergreen are Regional Transportation District bus drivers who see their roles as extending beyond transportation and into child development. They've become grandparents to Coco and Gus. John Edwards got interested in the synagogue after hearing about it from Coco. Now he's a fixture, a dapper older man in a silver sharkskin western suit. (He's also a Christian, but that seldom comes up.) Ada Jones, who drives the afternoon shift, calls me at least once a month to discuss the politics at Coco's high school—whether Coco is getting caught up with the wrong crowd, why she was so upset last week, how we can get her grades up. She'll pop by the high school to deliver all the things Coco forgets—her lunch, her cello, and, once, her bra. And what will Gus wear for Halloween? I have pictures of all three of my dogs sitting in Ada's bus. She likes the company.

Last Christmas, Coco gave John Edwards a copy of *The Joys of Yiddish*. Its content quickly trickled down to the other drivers.

"This morning at the bus barn," Ada said, "I called John Edwards a little schmuck and he said, 'I'd prefer you call me a *big* schmuck.'" Next day it was snowing hard, and she was late picking up Gus. Traffic and low visibility, she said, and other *mishegass*. And now when John Edwards sees us, he yells "*Shalom aleichem*" out the window.

10:30 A.M.

Rabbi Jamie hands me the *yod*, the little silver hand with which we mark our place on the Torah, because if you touched it with your fingers, the oils would eat away the fragile lambskin. My mouth and eyes are dry and my hand is shaking. *Please. This would be a shitty time to poke a hole in the Torah, as if there ever were a good one.*

I learned my portion from Joanne, who made me a tape months and months ago. "It's a good one," she said then. "It has the sixty curses, which the Orthodox like to read double time because they find it disturbing and unpleasant."

The curses are excellently specific: "The Lord will strike you with the Egyptian inflammation, with hemorrhoids, boil-scars and itch, from which you shall never recover."

"The portion you picked fits your own story," Rabbi Jamie told me at our first official meeting. "It's Moses telling the story to a whole new generation of Jews who have been wandering the desert for forty years. 'When you enter the Promised Land,' he's saying, 'what kinds of goals are you going to set yourself?' Every

Jew is obliged to be a teacher, and this is what you'll teach us about. Yours is the story that leads up to the point of making the covenant, which is the covenant your ancestors made, even though, in your case, there was an interruption."

There was. Neither my grandfather nor my father believed in God, and they had no desire to be Jews. But now that they weren't around to stand up for themselves, I no longer saw them as all that *goyish*.

In fact, my cousin Lisa, utterly enmeshed in the family archive since Aunt Cookie died, recently tapped a vein of Chotzie's essays, written long ago, which show him to be more connected to the Jews of Europe than I would have thought. But then, why wouldn't he have been? At the beginning of the group of writings Lisa likes to call "Chotzie vs. Nazi," the atmosphere he reports is so foreign—people seemed to think of Hitler as a political curiosity. Of course, you didn't have to be Jewish to feel the foreboding, but there's no getting around the fact that my grandfather did. Here's what he wrote in 1934:

Recently I traveled to Third Avenue and Ninety-Sixth Street to see the German film "S. A. Mann Brand." The picture is advertised as 100% Nazi, and the percentage is not exaggerated. I hate to give it a free ad, but there is just the chance that knowledge of its whereabouts and its content will send a lot of people, who have not made up their minds about the Third Reich, to see it. No person with the smallest grain of sense will, after seeing it, hesitate to make up his mind. In fact, "S. A. Mann Brand" could be indorsed with profit by Jews, Communists, Catholics and

whatever other minorities have a stake in the ultimate destruc-
tion of Hitlerism . . .

Only a handful of people saw the showing with me. They were
all Aryans, unmistakably. . . . According to the film, the German
nation was driven to the swastika through the fear of Communism
and the industrial power of the Jews.

Like all Jews, Chotzie and my father were fond of expounding on their lives—they built up legends and extended families, related by blood and more tenuous ties, and survived injustice.

They believed in individualism, which made them bigger. Their personalities helped them take up more of the world. I believe in God, which helps me take up less, although perhaps I'm more part of the world. But we all love our stories—and as Rami Shapiro says, all religion is, is a story.

They valued justice just a little more than forgiveness, which justified all that not-speaking-to-each-other. But often, in true Yom Kippur spirit, they wiped the slate clean. My father was so adept at pissing people off, yet so willing to apologize. We once had a vicious argument about oil-field machinery, of all things, and he followed it with a blistering letter informing me that I was no longer his daughter. I immediately sent back a handwritten letter—I couldn't care less about being disowned, and furthermore, I could prove he was wrong. Mere seconds after receiving my letter, he called. He couldn't read my handwriting, or my insults. This brought us to an impasse.

"So," he finally said, "did you eat yet?" The tension evaporated and we went out for lunch.

Both of them had an entirely Jewish view of mitzvahs—that doing good should feel good. My father raised money for the Colorado Symphony because he liked symphonies, and besides, this one let him sneak in through the back door to play poker with the musicians.

And there's no question that he believed in *that which is happening now.* It kept him from having to save up for Marina's college education. It reminded him to go outside, observe the squirrels, and perfect the art of doing nothing. It helped him justify mail-order caviar.

He wallowed in life and its potential for unimagined riches. I think of him whenever I sing my *haftarah,* which is basically a catalog of exciting prizes available to good Jews—the usual gold and silver, domination of lesser peoples, precious herbs, world peace. But it also promises camels—not just one or two, but *dust clouds of camels!* My father's version would be the magical Suburban, as well as anything else with an engine that could constitute his heart's desire.

One day he took a cab home from the hospital—he'd been there at least a week—and went directly out to the garage, tottering behind his all-wheel-drive walker, to start up his motorcycle. The girl who was living with him at the time, the renter he never bothered to charge rent, called me in a panic.

"He's out in the garage," she said. "He could do anything. Aren't you worried? He could be such a danger to other motorists!"

If he ever got out of the garage, I thought, but he didn't, being far too weak to move so much as a kickstand. But there's something about the mere sound of a motorcycle engine turning over that screams *l'chaim!*

My Torah portion is more than the covenant. It's also a series of rules—how Israel would run its life when it could finally settle down and grow things: . . . *you shall take some of every first fruit of the soil, which you harvest from the land that the Lord your God is giving you. . . . The Priest shall take the basket . . . and set it down in front of the altar of the Lord your God.*

"And the entire Torah ends, by the way, without the Jews getting into the garden," Rabbi Jamie observed. "And we go back to the beginning again, to the original garden. It's a book for a community in exile, with always the hope and the expectation that we'll be in the garden someday."

"No kidding," I said. "I've been trying to grow a ripe tomato here for ten years, and I still can't do it."

"And you may never get to the garden," Jamie said. "Then what?"

Ellen Diesenhof's husband, Marty, says, "Remember, there's nothing holy about chanting. The notes are just ways to remember what you're doing. To remind you to keep going. The Christians and the Muslims do it, too."

All Jews do it a little differently. All of us who care about that sort of thing stare at the cryptic marks that appear over and under the Hebrew consonants and vowels, trying to surmise how they're supposed to sound. A lot of my fellow chanters at Beth Evergreen swear by a computer program called Trope Trainer, but I stick with Joanne Greenberg's method. She figured all this out forty years ago in a rock quarry, and I decided to do what she did, among my own rocks.

At this point, I can sing the Torah portion in my sleep, yet it wakes me up at night, runs in the subconscious parts of my brain, and escapes my lips as I wash dishes or turn the compost. As long as I remember to sing it slowly and refuse to be shy, I'll be fine. I think of my father then: *Operatic? I'll show you operatic. Whaddaya think, old man?*

I move to the *haftarah*, a long poem by Isaiah that begins with *kumi o'ri*, or "rise and shine." It's taken me half a year to learn four pages, listening to a tape recorded long ago by Cantor Israel Yannai, somewhere in midtown Manhattan. (You can hear the muted sounds of taxi horns in the background.) I was never able to learn more than a paragraph a day, but every week I lurched forward a little further. Meditation based on deep breathing—the big frustration of my Buddhist days—became unavoidable. In order to chant, I guess, you have to keep your breath going. Rather than untangle the words when you're right on top of them, you have to look ahead to the next phrase, as you do with rocks and trees on the path when mountain biking or snowboarding. When a stray thought rambled into my head while chanting *haftarah*, I sent it away, gently, and it went. And whenever my practice session ended I felt genuinely cleansed.

11:00 A.M.

I begin the *d'var torah,* which translates as "interpretation of the text," but has come to mean "the speech in which I thank everyone and say what I learned" at these events.

"I should now say a little about my Torah portion," I read, "and what we might learn from it. But I don't know what *we* might learn. I have little experience with *we,* although it's become an interest of mine."

Of course I end with "thank you for coming," but my eyes are so glazed over I can't seem to look directly at anyone. *Colorado,* I think, *is awfully dry,* and then I realize I'm missing the Proud Parent Speech, which is being given by Eric and Coco.

Coco remembers the time a few months ago when I was driving her to cheerleading practice and absolutely lost it in the car, in hysterics because I was sure I could *never* get it together enough to survive a bat mitzvah. Eric remembers my father—how annoyed he would be by all this hoo-ha, but how willing he would have been, in the end, to assume his place as the head of the *mishpoche.* Eric suspects that my interest in faith will be as contagious as my love of mariachi music and gardening. It's not a bit unpleasant to hear my husband and daughter say how much they love me, in public.

As the service ends, I'm wondering how things stand between me and God after this big, big event. Some people get married over and over again, but this, after all, I will do only once. Then it's over and I'm looking around for my official certificate and my reading glasses and my shoes, which I took off hours ago for fear of teetering, and I help put the prayer books away and go into the social hall to join in the blessing over bread and wine. At that point the mystery shrinks away. God and I will just continue, as before. I'm an adult Jew now. There will always be plenty to do.

Noon

I come home to a mountainside covered with Jews—old ladies in high heels trying to make it up the driveway, little girls chasing my dogs around. Marina has set out the hummus, muhammara, tabouleh, and the wonderful stuff she calls "fig goo." Eric is in the backyard grilling lamb. Proceeding directly to the sangria, I drink a big glass in one gulp. I change out of my dress and into my favorite jeans. I start to feel normal again.

Normal conversation flows through the house. Some people think I kicked ass—that I'm a good teacher of Judaism and a perfectly acceptable piano player. Others are there, I see, to stand in for my father.

"Jesus, Rob," says his old friend Ray, "I was bracing myself for everyone to start singing 'Kumbaya.'" But then he gives me a fountain pen. "It was either that or a Timex watch," he says.

"Robin. Your brown dog is nipping at some little kid. The kid was pulling its tail, but still."

"Robin. Your white dog is eating chocolate chip cookies off the dining room table."

"Robin," Eric says. "Did you eat?"

Of course! Eat! Grilled haloumi cheese and baklava oozing honey. More sangria. When people talk to me I just stare happily at them. I think I'm getting even for my first wedding, when I was so worried about whether my guests were getting along. Was the music any good? Could they tell my vital organs were being slowly crushed to death inside the corset from hell?

Now I don't care. I hope they have fun. I think they will. I think I'll drink more sangria and smile at the rabbi. I think I'll feel this free forever, a sweet feeling. But I know I won't, which makes it even sweeter.

Jenny emerges from the bedroom in a costume made from small bits of fringe and a lot of naked skin. Thirteen-year-old boys have belly dancers at their parties—why not me? The crowd is thrown to the edges of the living room by her centrifugal force. Ada and her girlfriend Linda sit with their mouths open. Jenny pulls me out onto the impromptu dance floor and I undulate around a little, not caring if I look stupid. Another serious advantage of waiting so long to come of age.

How good and pleasant it is to be a forty-seven-year-old bat mitzvah.

4:00 P.M.

A dozen of us remain at the party. Marina is doing Coco's hair for tonight's homecoming dance. The phone's beginning to ring—high-school friends pre-gossiping about the night to come. The rest of us decide to shake off the day by hiking up the mountain behind our house, which is owned by a guy named Mr. Og, who lives in Arizona. We've never met him, but he gave us e-mail permission to roam his land. In a strange coincidence, I spent the past year learning to chant a Hebrew text that includes the story of how King Og and King Sihon tried to overrun the Jews, but were bitterly defeated: "We took their land and gave it to Reubenites . . . "

"It's the same story, over and over again," Joanne said. "Once we get a victory, we never stop talking about it."

The ancient tune of the *haftarah* runs through my head as I walk up through the ponderosa and cactus. Then I hear the first elk bugle of the season, wheezing in the distance like a broken accordion. The High Holy Days are only a week away.

11:00 P.M.

Everyone's asleep, even the two hyperactive sisters who came to spend the night with Gus. I can't stop thinking about growing something. I want to build a greenhouse and try, once more, to grow a tomato. My Hebrew name is Chava, which means Eve, the woman who spent her early years messing around in a garden. I don't know where I'll get the construction materials or how to use them, but I absolutely won't accept living in a desert for the foreseeable future. If I have to, I'll string ten-foot vinyl fencing and chicken wire until my garden looks like a prison camp and my neighbors, whose idea of paradise is very different from mine, complain. With a jackhammer and hardware cloth I'll run a barrier one foot into the ground to keep out the chipmunks. Sage, mint, foxglove—smelly or poisonous plants that critters know enough to keep away from. Not only will I do this, I'll start tomorrow, because the day after that I might die in a freak car–elk accident. I'm wound up, I know.

Still, you have to try to cultivate something in this world, not the next. I can hardly say how Jewish that sounds to me.

There's only one thing left to do before bed—find the *Etz Chayim* and another well-used cassette tape of a guy singing in Hebrew. I agreed to chant some of the *haftarah* for Rosh Hashanah next week, and I should probably get started.

It's another interesting story—about Hannah, who was married to a good man but wasn't happy because "the Lord had closed her womb," and she desperately wanted a child. Finally, she went to supplicate before a priest, saying, "O Lord of Hosts, if you will look upon your maidservant and . . . if you will grant me a male child, I will dedicate him to the Lord for all the days of his life . . ." It was a sincere prayer, but she said it so quietly that the priest only saw her lips moving, and he thought she was drunk, and she had to convince him otherwise. She continued to talk to God, and eventually she got the son she wanted and praised the Lord in perfect matriarchal poetry: "My heart exults in the LORD; / I have triumphed through the LORD. / I gloat over my enemies!"

Tonight I'll learn the first line. The rest will follow. For a while, Hannah will become the person I think about when I'm alone, trying to understand her, whether or not she speaks directly to me, and what her story means now, as opposed to thousands of years ago. There will certainly be no shortage of Jews who'll want to discuss it: *Why so anxious for a boy, Hannah? A girl would be such a disappointment?*

I won't forget Hannah even when I start singing about someone else. She's my ancestor, my eccentric relative. Sometimes I think they all are.

Acknowledgments

Though I desperately wanted to write this book, I wasn't sure I could accomplish a beginning, middle, and end. My editor, Lisa Kaufman, diffused the *tsuris* with the words "Oh, we can fix that." I've depended on her ever since. My agent, Betsy Amster, acted as mensch-on-demand, as she always does. Joanne Greenberg and Ellen and Marty Diesenhof apparently saw me as their mitzvah project, a hell of a deal for me.

No other synagogue is anything like Congregation Beth Evergreen is, and I'm grateful to everyone who ever walked through its doors. In particular, I thank Neshama Mousseau, Carrie Urban, Jill Wildenberg, and Phil Zeitler, and I'm scared to death of having left someone out.

Rabbi Elliot Baskin opened the door. Rabbi Rami Shapiro flung it wide open. And as for Rabbi Jamie Arnold—he can sing, dance, promulgate Torah, ski, *and* snowboard. Both irreverent and reverent, he's the best kind of spiritual teacher. Luckily for all of his, he married Marti, who is smart, funny, and kind.

It's embarrassing to admit that my mental, physical, and financial fitness during the writing of this book was almost entirely accomplished by other people. Rich Bell, Tim Buese, Claire

DaRoca, Nancy Masten, and Carrie Sclar acted as trainers. Kat Allen, Tony Hutchins, and Toby Threadgill, non-Jews, talked to me about religion when I was thirsty for such things. Sam Gary, Bill Strickland, and Kyle Wagner gave me work I not only needed but enjoyed tremendously.

My cousin Lisa Grossman served as a one-woman, fine-tooth-comb research department. My uncle Herbert Grossman was no slouch either. Louise Redd knows her writing and overhauled mine. She did it with such finesse and sensitivity that I still wanted to drink champagne with her when it was over.

In a peculiar way, I wrote this book in memory of my father, Blair Chotzinoff, even when he was still alive. But now more than ever.

My elite corps of relatives never ran out of support and empathy: Ryan Dirksen, Sarah Dirksen, and Nick Selvy.

My sister Marina Chotzinoff is absolutely necessary. If you knew her, you couldn't do without her either.

You should also wish you had a husband like Eric Dexheimer, but there is only one of him. Every day since he came to me I have thanked God, even when I didn't know who I was thanking.